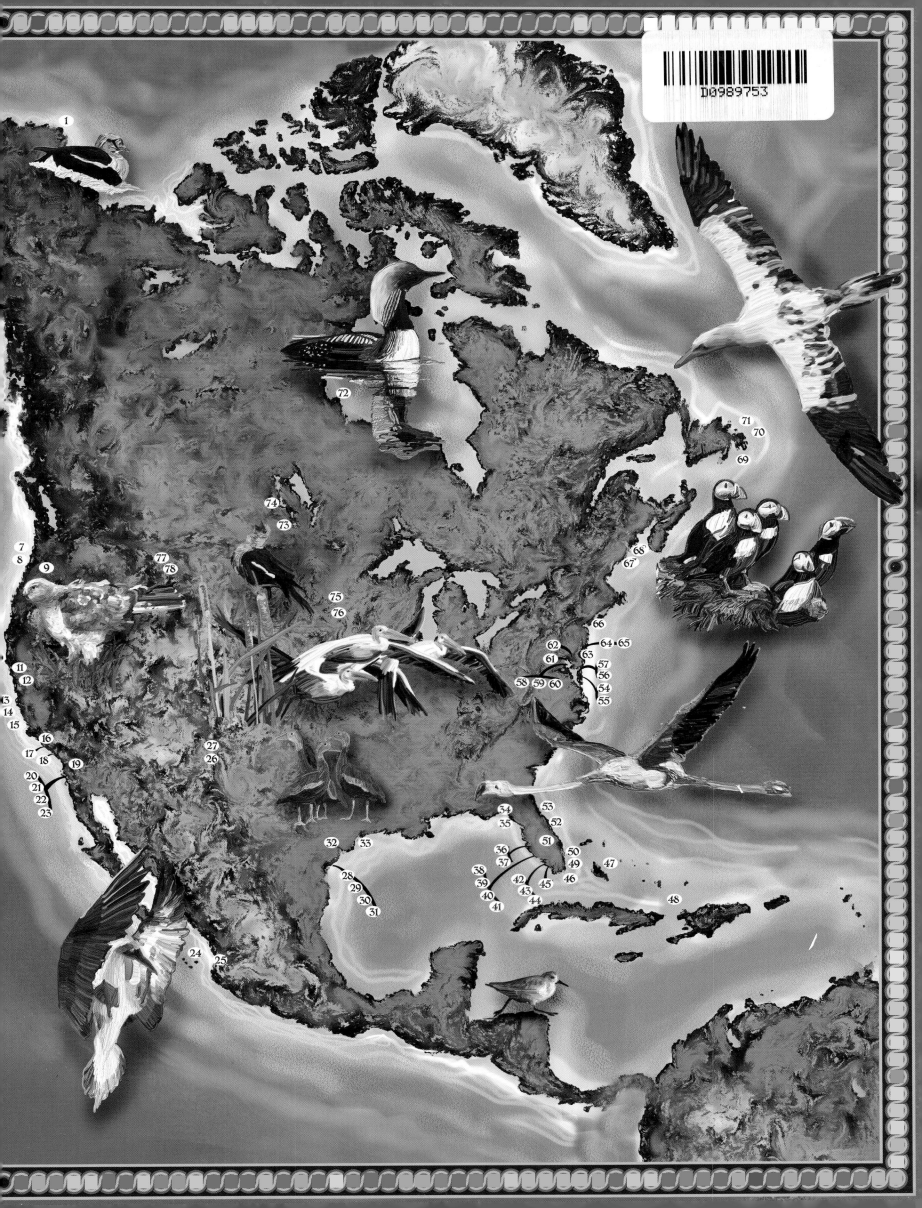

A Celebration of
North American
Waterbirds

RHAPSODY IN BLUE

A Celebration of
North American Waterbirds

PHOTOGRAPHY BY MIDDLETON EVANS

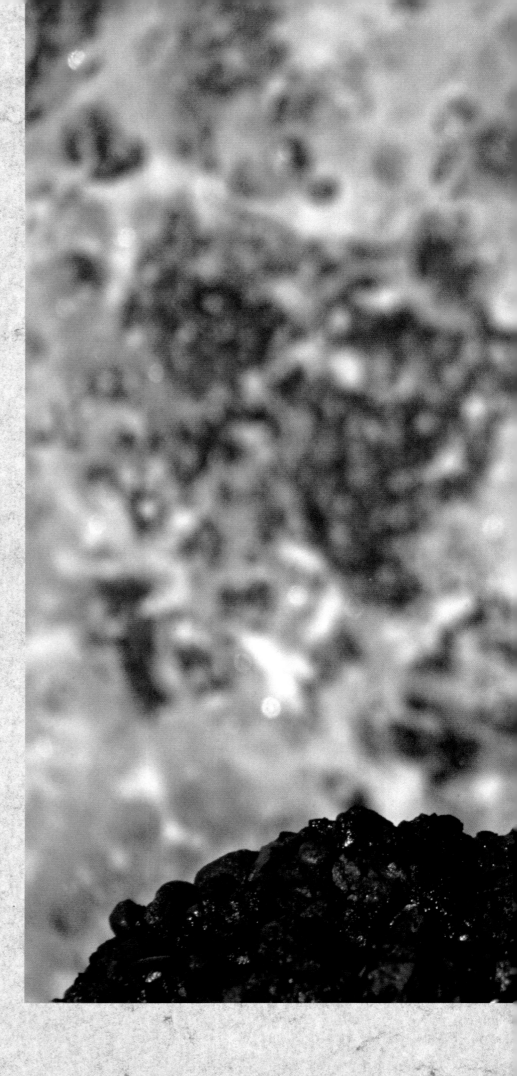

Rhapsody in Blue
A Celebration of North American Waterbirds

Photography by Middleton Evans

RAVENWOOD PRESS

Ravenwood Press
PO Box 496
Fallston, Maryland 21047-0496
Phone 410-877-2432 / 1-800-807-1079
Fax 410-877-2419
www.ravenwoodpress.com

Text and book design by Middleton Evans
Cover Design by Patrick Reid O'Brien
Typography and graphic production by Elizabeth Davidson
High-resolution film scanning by Andrew Hall
Text Formulation & Preliminary Scanning by Kristie Evans
Printing by Pacifica Communications

Permission for materials quoted on page 271.

Printed in Korea
First Edition April 2007

Library of Congress Control Number: 2006928818

ISBN 978-09778055-1-8

Page 1: A feeding Reddish Egret at Florida's Estero Lagoon strikes a provocative pose while stirring up minnows at sunset.

Page 2: The gnarled wood of an ancient cypress tree makes a fitting stage for a stately Great Blue Heron at Wakulla Springs on Florida's panhandle.

Page 4: An immature Bald Eagle transforms driftwood into art along Kachemak Bay, framed by pristine mountains on Alaska's Kenai Peninsula.

Page 6: Competing drake Wood Ducks face off on a freshly-leafed tree harboring a prime nesting cavity in Maryland's Patterson Park.

Page 8: A flock of brilliant Roseate Spoonbills settle in for the evening amidst tangled mangrove at J.N. "Ding" Darling NWR on Florida's gulf coast.

Page 10: Nesting brown boobies investigate a stranger in their midst on Isabel Island, a thriving seabird sanctuary off Mexico's Pacific Coast.

Page 12: Winged Snow Geese and Sandhill Cranes are a daily winter spectacle at Bosque del Apache NWR, an oasis along New Mexico's Rio Grande.

Page 14: Half-way along spring migration to tundra breeding grounds, a Dunlin pauses for a wing stretch at Stone Harbor in southern New Jersey.

Page 15: A Black Oystercatcher relies on dextrous feet to navigate surf-sprayed boulders at Point Lobos on California's magnificent coast.

CHAPTER ONE

The
PortaitGallery

CHAPTER TWO

Flights of
Fancy

CHAPTER THREE

Three Square
Meals

Dedication

I wish to dedicate this book to my wife, Kristie Edwards Evans, for the past seven wonderful years of adventure, support, love, and growth. I admire your deep appreciation of nature and your courage to seek new horizons. Your enthusiasm for these photographs, and for the Rhapsody project in general have encouraged me to push forward thru the peaks and valleys with my dreams. Your countless hours with preliminary scans and text formation have been a tremendous gift to this project. I am grateful for your companionship on trips to Florida, Maine, California and Alaska. Thanks for letting me share my knowledge of the birds I passionately photograph. I wish you worlds of joy and success on your unique journey. Long live the golden goose. Namaste.

Acknowledgements

First and foremost, I would like to praise God for creating this world's infinite beauty, especially the feathered gems that have enthralled me for a lifetime. Your love, patience and artistic genius knows no bounds. I am eternaly gratefull for the life, teachings, and ultimate sacrifice of Jesus so that we could know a better way. ❦ A heartfelt thanks to my parents, Bob and Shiny Evans, and my late grandmother, Gertrude Black, who have been extraordinarily supportive of my career. ❦ To Bob Rinker, a world of thanks for being so enthusiastic about this project, and for helping me find such glorious birds on our trips near and far. ❦ To Rhonda Kidd, thanks for the memories of experiencing nature at the continent's four corners. ❦ To Jessica Earle, your companionship on trips out west enriched the experience—keep up the great work with your camera. ❦ To Jean Keene, you make the dreams of bird photographers come true. Thank you for sharing these magnificent eagles with me and the rest of the world! ❦ A special thank you to Arthur Morris, whose relentless pursuit of artistic perfection has inspired me to reach for new horizons. Your leadership on seven photo tours and willingness to share valuable information represent an extraordinary generosity. ❦ A number of other individuals made sterling contributions to hook me up with my dream birds during this five-year odyssey. Without your kindness, *Rhapsody* would not have been possible. They include: Gerda Deterer, Ralph Paonessa, Kevin Karlson, Tom Soucek, Moose Peterson, Dave Brinker, Verena Gill, Robin Cole, Harry Harris, Lisa and Bryan Glorioso, Jim Freible, Ben Gilbreath, Basil Kelly, Lynn Gape, Dr. Peter Beamish, Madeline Link, Lee Greenly, Casey Greenly, Bill Smylie, Greg Gillson, Barna Norton, John Norton, Joe Ondek, Armando Santiago, Dr. Cliff Oliver and Steven Emmons. ❦ A heartfelt thanks to my dream team on the production side: Cecile Caronna of Pacifica Communications, an outstanding production manager (printing broker) ❦ Elizabeth Davidson of Baseline Graphics (typography & design implementation) ❦ Patrick Reid O'Brien of OB Design (map & cover design) ❦ Andrew Hall of Harrison Photographic (film scanning) ❦ Each of you represents the best of your trade with unparalleled professionalism. Working with you is a pleasure. Continued success to all of you!

Rhapsody in Blue

As fate would have it, a muskrat picked the worst possible spot to surface, and my life path was headed into unchartered territory. It was March 1998 at Oscar Scherer State Park near Tampa. My shooting buddy, Bob Rinker, and I were working a beautiful Florida Scrub-Jay at the picnic area when a commotion at the adjacent lake caught the eye of my friend. One look through the camera revealed a toothy rodent in dire straits, trapped in a Great Blue Heron vise. We approached with caution and awe. Fortunately, the hungry bird was too preoccupied to pay us much attention. Perhaps this heron overestimated his elasticity, as it struggled to swallow the muskrat. We managed to fire off a roll or two before the bird flew into a thicket, muskrat in tow.

What a way to kick off our Florida birding marathon! Little did I know that every day would be as good as the last, a parade of thrilling photo-ops almost too good to be true. Highlights include close encounters with the splendid Purple Gallinule and the secretive Least Bittern at Wakodahatchee Wetlands near Boynton Beach. A missed exit in Venice put us on a near collision course with a pair of Sandhill Cranes crossing the highway by foot, in no particular hurry, to feed in a wet depression next to a Denny's. Courting wading birds delighted a whole battalion of photographers at both the Venice and St. Augustine rookeries. At Merritt Island, Black-necked Stilts mated not 30 yards from our car—quite an acrobatic feat for such ungainly creatures. Let's not forget the white morph Reddish Egret at Estero Lagoon on Fort Myers Beach. A three-day search for this oddity was proving unsuccessful, though many other birds were easily photographed. We were just about to head back to the hotel when a large white bird (presumably a Great Egret) landed right in front of me. Once I got a good look at the pink breeding lores, there was no doubt as to its identity. Then this southern belle proceeded to pluck minnows from the shallows. I couldn't have scripted it better in a dream, ten days of heaven on Earth. A new chapter in my life was unfolding.

By 1998, my 12-year career as a Maryland photographer was in full bloom. I had three books published, one on Baltimore and two on Maryland. Initially, I documented the cultural landscape of Maryland—festivals, cities and towns, sporting traditions, recreation, lifestyles and the arts. In 1992, with six years of professional experience under my belt, I started work on my first collection of nature photographs. Equally enthralled with spiders and toads as with bears and eagles, I criss-crossed my home state for nearly four years in search of nature's bounty. I also met many wonderful people who

kindly shared special places for me to visit. Released in 1996, *Maryland's Great Outdoors* was the culmination of a life-long passion for wild things.

All of my hard work reaped quite an unexpected dividend in 1999. Maryland Public Television selected me as one of six distinguished local photographers of the twentieth century to be featured in the Emmy Award-winning documentary, *Images of Maryland: 1900-2000*. I was especially honored to be included with A. Aubrey Bodine, a Maryland legend whose artistic work inspired me more than any other individual. I love his painterly compositions with perfectly balanced elements that draw viewers inside and keep them there. Lacquered with a coat of sentimentality, his images chronicle a half-century of Maryland history.

With a good flow in my career, I decided to start a second book on Baltimore in 1997. The first edition had sold out, and a second wave of rejuvenation was lapping at the Patapsco's banks. The trip to Florida was intended to be a fun break during the halfway point of the Baltimore project. Yet, when I returned, thoughts of charming festivals, handsome buildings, and cozy neighborhoods were usurped by soaring eagles, dancing cranes and preening spoonbills. The birds had won over my heart, and the treasures of Charm City would have to wait for another day.

I decided to return to Florida, as there was unfinished business at the St. Augustine Alligator Farm. By April, the first Great Egret chicks would be hatching while the smaller waders would be courting in earnest. Sure enough, the Tricolored Herons and Snowy and Cattle Egrets were strutting their stuff within feet of the boardwalk that crosses the big alligator pond. An early-morning run to Merritt Island to search for that stilt nest yielded Black Skimmers feeding in a shallow pool by the road. This was the perfect opportunity to put my new Nikon 600mm f4 autofocus lens to the test. Skimmers feed on the wing, lower mandible slicing across the smooth surface on a collision course with minnows... not a job for the manual focus lens. I shot several laps of birds fishing, some almost filling the frame. Most of the images were tack sharp and I was delighted with my new lens.

This second trip to Florida drew me further into the dream. I do not recall the exact moment when this book was conceived, but the transition from fantasy to drawing board was well underway. The seeds were planted five years prior with

the *Maryland's Great Outdoors* project. Of the many subjects that I pursued, the waterbirds most nourished my soul. I have always been drawn to the edges where land meets water; growing up in Maryland there was plenty of opportunity for that. Mix in some beautiful birds and I am very much at peace, with not a care in the world.

One final experience was the exclamation point that I needed to commit whole-heartedly to the project. Within a week of returning from St. Augustine, I was hired to photograph a tugboat in Northern Virginia. I left a day early to make a stop at Ocean City, Maryland, as the inlet jetty had been productive for unusual birds in prior years. Pulling into a parking lot by the jetty, I noticed a distant group of ducks... perhaps they were beautiful Long-tailed Ducks. Focusing my binoculars on them, I was shocked to see a bird that I had never seen before—the striking Harlequin Duck, a rarity on the New England coast, and almost unheard of south of the Mason-Dixon Line. That afternoon and the next morning, I carefully maneuvered into position, crouching behind a knee-high cinderblock wall at the Jetty Motel. The skittish birds acclimated to my presence and hauled out on some sunlit boulders. My hands trembled with excitement, as I could not believe that these rare ducks were being so accommodating. Upon reviewing the film, the deal was closed—I was going to do a North American waterbirds book, and it was time to make some plans. The project was code-named "Waterwings" and served as the initial title of the book until *Rhapsody in Blue* caught my fancy five years later.

Brainstorming at every free moment, my imagination ran wild. Articles from *Birder's World*, *Wild Bird*, and *Outdoor Photographer* magazines were no longer the stuff of daydreams, but now reference material. I would finally go to all those mythical places—Bosque del Apache NWR, Churchill, The Everglades, and the Pribilof Islands to name a few. Images flashed through my mind, recalling countless coffeetable books, Discovery Channel programs, and a basement full of *National Geographics*. Extraordinary moments include Western Grebes dancing across a lake in nuptial bliss, a blizzard of Snow Geese blasting off from a cornfield, puffins stuffing their bills with fish, and the cartoonish antics of loafing pelicans. Surely, these

would have to be in the book. Studying my growing collection of nature books, I was surprised to learn how many birds I did not know. I was familiar with most of the North American wading birds and waterfowl, but had only seen a handful during my Maryland romps. Limpkins and the bitterns were alluring... so were the Hooded Merganser and King Eider, most dapper of the drakes. Many of the shorebird species were new to me, and I would have to seek them out. Wetland raptors were also a must... would I ever photograph the male Northern Harrier, an alluring bird that stirs deep in my soul. Majestic Bald Eagles and reclusive Snail Kites—I would have to find a way to get close. Open-ocean seabirds were also a mystery to me in 1998, but I would travel the continent to make their acquaintance. I even hoped to see an albatross.

Imagine a big coffeetable book, artistically designed, with all of these colorful characters and amazing behaviors. I had never seen anything like it, and that was the book that was begging to be done. Exuberant at the thought of all these pictures in my mind, I was equally daunted by the enormous effort required to pull it off. At the outset, many questions were unanswered. How would I find all of my target species in the wild? Could I get close enough to make decent images? Would the weather cooperate during my scheduled trips? Would my health hold up? Chronic asthma has always weakened my strength and endurance. How would I pay for all of this?

Timeout! Take a deep breath. Like any undertaking in life, it could only be done one step at a time, one day at a time. During the seven years that this project consumed me, I would learn profound things about myself, the spirit of a wild creature, and God—before 1998 only a stranger to me. Most importantly, I came to realize that it doesn't matter if there is a pot of gold at the end of the rainbow. The journey itself is life's greatest gift, living each day to its fullest, filled with wonder and adventure, taking joy from everyday blessings, and mustering the courage and faith to chase my dreams.

By May 1998, I was committed full-throttle to the project, despite all the uncertainty. My strategy was to sign up for photo workshops in prime locations led by distinguished photographers, capitalizing on their intimate knowledge of an area. My first big trip would be to Churchill on the Canadian tundra, most famous for its polar bears. During the brief arctic summer, numerous species of waterbird nest in the short grasses, a vibrant canvas brought to life with nesting's high drama. While searching for a guide in a magazine, I stumbled across an ad for Lake Manitoba birding. The guide, Harry Harris, informed me that he had access to an American White Pelican colony, which sounded promising, so I signed up for this leg of my big Canadian adventure. It started out well enough, meeting our captain with his 20-foot motorboat at the end of a dirt road. En route to the distant pelican colony, we stopped at a few islands, including a Ring-billed Gull colony with chicks in various stages of hatching. Another spot yielded a clutch of freshly-hatched Canada Geese. Speeding to the great rookery, we noticed that a small portion of Lake Manitoba had found its way into the boat, which we attempted to bail out. The wind started to kick-up;

the bumpy, wet and chilly ride was now rather ominous as the skies darkened. Despite our vigorous bailing the boat was slowly sinking in the middle of a lake as big as Baltimore County. My heart sank faster than a lead sinker.

We pulled up to the nearest island, unloaded all the gear, and prayed that the captain could make it back to shore with a lightened load to repair the leak or secure another boat. At this point in my life, my comfort zone was still pretty small, and not being a man of faith, my thoughts slipped into a dark void. The hours passed, with little food and no shelter or means of communication. What was I doing stranded in the Canadian wilderness? I could be finishing up my Baltimore book, photographing the coronation of a new big-haired diva at the Café Hon (remember John Waters' kitschy movie *Hairspray*)? The spin-cycle of doubts in my mind was finally broken by the faint drone of a distant motor. Our captain had another boat! It was decided that we still had enough daylight to make a run for the colony.

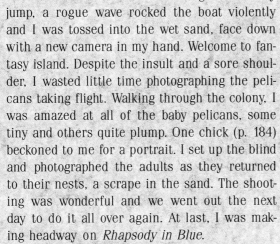

Approaching the island, I saw hundreds of the giant white birds covering every section of bare ground interspersed with obsidian cormorants. I stood on the bow laden with equipment eager for landfall. Just as I lifted one leg to start my jump, a rogue wave rocked the boat violently and I was tossed into the wet sand, face down with a new camera in my hand. Welcome to fantasy island. Despite the insult and a sore shoulder, I wasted little time photographing the pelicans taking flight. Walking through the colony, I was amazed at all of the baby pelicans, some tiny and others quite plump. One chick (p. 184) beckoned to me for a portrait. I set up the blind and photographed the adults as they returned to their nests, a scrape in the sand. The shooting was wonderful and we went out the next day to do it all over again. At last, I was making headway on *Rhapsody in Blue*.

With a few good shots under my belt, I was off to Churchill to meet up with Moose Peterson and his group. Looking out the plane over the vast tundra, I felt like I had traveled to the ends of the Earth. The Hudson Bay was a sea of mini-icebergs stretched to the horizon. My God! What was a pampered city boy doing up here?

After seeing all of those articles on Churchill filled with gorgeous close-up photos of birds nesting in clumps of tundra wildflowers, I thought that this was going to be a walk-in-the-park. Driving in the van for hours at a time, day after day, finally seeing a bird to photograph, only to have it fly away after rigging up our gear, now this was downright depressing. The gloomy cloudy skies didn't help either. Fortunately, a couple of birds gave us a few close looks, including a Hudsonian Godwit, Pacific Loon, Arctic Tern, and a Long-tailed Duck. Although the photography was disappointing, I was grateful to have had the chance to experience the sub-arctic and the fragile lives of its inhabitants. I also realized that this book project was going to kick my butt.

I had barely enough time to review my slides when it was time to pack my bags for another trip, an instructional photo tour with Arthur Morris to Alaska's Pribilofs. St. Paul Island would prove to be just as foreign, alluring, and mysterious as Churchill. Situated halfway between the Alaskan mainland and Russia, St. Paul's craggy cliffs are home to over a million seabirds—auklets, murres, puffins, kittiwakes, cormorants, and fulmars. The landscape is hauntingly beautiful; a rippled, tree-less terrain of green grasses interspersed with blue carpets of wild lupines and other flowers. Fog banks roll over the island in waves, and visibility can change drastically from hour to hour. Northern fur seals blanket sections of rocky beach while crafty arctic foxes deftly maneuver along the clifftops in search of an unsuspecting seabird. It sounds like paradise. After reading such descriptions, I had to check it out for myself.

Unlike Churchill, getting close to the birds was not a problem, but getting a clean, unobstructed view was very much a problem, as we were shooting down from the clifftops. Sometimes a puffin would be just five feet below you, but you could barely make out the head through overhanging grasses. On one such occasion a Horned Puffin (p. 230) was right under my nose. However, to get a good angle, I had to lie on my belly and lean over the edge, my chest freely suspended over the rocky beach 200 feet below. Amazingly, the bird did not flinch, and with a hand-held 400mm lens, I managed to shoot two rolls. After years of taking no risks, I was finally living life on the edge, releasing many of my fears. I had never felt so alive! After a week of often arduous hikes to the best vantage points on the island, I was able to photograph all of the seabird species, and chalked up the trip as a great success.

By Thanksgiving of 1998, I had plenty to be thankful for, especially this wildly exciting new book project. At our family gathering, I projected my favorite bird slides. Their enthusiastic response only added fuel to my fire, as I jetted off to New Mexico the next day for an Arthur Morris tour of Bosque del Apache National Wildlife Refuge. This legendary birding hotspot plays host to thousands of wintering Snow Geese and Sandhill Cranes, among others. For years, I had been hearing of this desert oasis and I was eager to see what all of the fuss was about. I did

not have to wait long. That first morning we were treated to a gorgeous sunrise as flocks of geese lifted off from an impoundment with a backdrop of pink and gold. For three straight days, the shooting never let up: postcard sunrises and sunsets, cranes and geese constantly moving about the refuge, and nice looks at raptors, ducks, blackbirds, and marauding coyotes. Sculpted mountains surround the valley and make for sweet backdrops.

During this part of my life, I had begun a spiritual awakening, and this Bosque experience felt like a warm embrace from Mother Earth, encouraging me to continue my journey. I knew that I would be returning someday, and two years later, I did. If only everyone could have this experience, I cannot help but think that the world would be a more peaceful and loving place.

After Christmas, it was time to pack up for what would be my longest trip of the project, a three-week West Coast odyssey in January. While in the Pribilofs, I met a fellow who talked of the famous eagle lady of Homer, Alaska, who feeds wild eagles daily in the winter. I called Jean and asked if I could stop by for a few days. My request was kindly granted and we were off to the great frozen north, armed with lots of batteries, film, and Polartec.

The first morning in Homer was surreal. En route to Jean's place, we passed a moose nibbling on branches behind a McDonald's. Once on the Homer spit, a long peninsula, I saw an eagle perched, oddly enough on a bait shop sign. Then they started to appear, eagles perched on snowbanks, fishing boats, huts, telephone poles, and houses. Eagles surrounded us... Alfred Hitchcock meets *Northern Exposure*.

Shortly thereafter, we met up with Jean for the daily eagle feeding. As soon as the first salmon fillets were thrown, the eagles rained in from every direction. With well over 100 eagles in shooting range, I was completely overwhelmed. One eagle would land on driftwood not 25 feet from me while two would fight over a salmon scrap. Another would perch

on the roof of her trailer so close that I could do head shots. Others would knock each other off prime perches. Meanwhile, my fingers were going numb (despite the doubled-up glove liners) and it was hard to focus as my eyes were tearing up from the icy wind. Talk about sensory overload! After an hour or two of bedlam, it ended as abruptly as it began, and the eagles flew off to their afternoon roosts. Fortunately, I had 22 hours to strategize for the next shoot, when, alas, the sun made a rare appearance. Instead of trying to get everything at once, I picked my shots carefully the next three days and was able to make nearly 50 special photographs culled from over 2,000 slides. Four years later, during the stretch run of this project, I returned to Homer with my wife, Kristie. Against all odds, we would meet five other photographers from Maryland in this coastal fishing village over 6,000 miles from home. Six sunny days of our seven translated into 250 rolls of film, most of it treasured flight images. Many thanks to Jean! Viva Homer!

The California leg of my West Coast odyssey in January 1999 was no less exciting. My first stop was the quaint fishing village of Bodega Bay, a few hours drive north of San Francisco. Here I received a treasured gift from the heavens—a male Northern Harrier, who allowed me to approach on foot from the road. As soon as he realized that I was locked on him, he stood up, ruffled his feathers, and said those all too familiar words, "I'm outta here." These few seconds with the Grey Ghost were a defining moment in my career as a wildlife photographer. With this kind of divine intervention, anything was possible and I might actually pull off the *Rhapsody in Blue* of my dreams.

The California trip reminded me of that fateful first trip to Florida—a marathon of new venues almost daily, with each spot yielding at least one big surprise. The Palo Alto Baylands offered a California Clapper Rail. Morro Bay harbored my first Red-throated Loon, beached by the receding tide. In Carmel, I strolled the beach with a rather friendly Whimbrel. In Monterey, Black Oystercatchers hopscotched on surf-sprayed boulders. Marbled Godwits fed right in front of me in Santa Barbara. Whoo-Ahh! I was in the zone. The drive down Highway 1 along Big Sur was breathtaking—and a little hairy, as only a skimpy guardrail prevented cars from careening over the precipitous cliffs. Approaching San Simeon, home to the opulent Hearst Castle, I noticed a gathering of people near the road and had to investigate. Elephant seals covered the beach; I was informed that this was a major birthing area and my timing was perfect. To add icing to the cake, numerous gulls had staked out the scene to feast on the afterbirth. For an instant, a Western Gull stared into the innocent eyes of a seal pup... nature at its finest—raw, unscripted and poignant.

To cap off the first year in style, I returned to Florida in late February 1999 for another 10-day marathon tour of the Gulf and Atlantic Coasts. As good as the first trip was, this one was even better. The real highlight of the trip was The Anhinga Trail in Everglades National Park. One lap around the trail and I knew that we had a top-ten North American waterbird hotspot. Anhingas nested in plain view of the boardwalk, attracted by the murky waters teeming with fish. Cormorants were also familiar with this fishing hole, and they gobbled up big fish all day long. Purple Gallinules danced across the lily pads, ever watchful of the abundant alligators. They say that history repeats itself, and I am a believer. Rinker called me on our walkie-talkies about a Great Blue Heron that had just caught a huge fish. I hoofed it down to the end of the trail where a large crowd had gathered, the birder's equivalent of the Super Bowl. People kindly made room for me to get a front-row seat, and the heron fumbled with this fish before swallowing it whole. Thank God I interviewed poorly for those banking jobs. This is the best job in the world.

This fabulous Florida marathon marked exactly one year into the project. It was better than my wildest dreams. I could have stopped here and put together a very nice book, but it was not the book that I signed on for. I was not even halfway down the list of all the compelling species, behaviors and habitats that beckoned me. I never intended to photograph every species of North American waterbird, but there were still so many capti-

vating ones from my research that I had to at least try to see in the wild. High on my list were the King Eider, American Flamingo, Red-billed Tropicbird, Snail Kite, Whooping Crane, Trumpeter Swan, Piping Plover, Pacific Golden-Plover, Atlantic Puffin, and Black-footed Albatross. Many others also enticed me. As time went on, I inevitably learned of all the North American species. The more I inquired, the more I realized that each and every species spoke to me. They are all unique, stunning in their own right, and each has a story of survival to tell.

By March of 1999, I did not know how or when the project would end; I trusted that when it was time to stop, I would just know in my heart. Looking at my ever-growing list, I knew that I had a long way to go. Now that I had hit the major hotspots where many species congregated, I now turned my attention to specific species and behaviors. My trips became increasingly specialized. Over the next three years, I would travel to many wonderful places, including Texas, Oregon, Maine, Montana, Newfoundland, Mexico, and the Bahamas. Florida, Alaska and California—the big three—were re-visited several times. The experiences and memories from these new adventures were no less wonderful than the first year. I was also transforming as a person, as the birds were teaching me valuable life lessons. More about that later...

At this juncture, I am not going to detail every trip. Nonetheless, in an effort to at least make mention of the myriad magical experiences from March 1998 to March 2003, I have added a "Photographic Notes" section, beginning on page 242. Beside a thumbnail of each photograph is a date, location, equipment used, and personal observations on making each shot. People often ask me how I get these kinds of pictures. Hopefully, this section will shed light on the trials and tribulations of a wildlife photographer.

There are two more trips that I would like to detail, however, as they really encapsulate the essence of this project—a jour-

ney into the unknown, a reunion with the divine. I stumbled across two very different islands in my research that proved irresistible. When I first saw a photo caption for Middleton Island in Mitsuaki Iwango's book *Wildlife*, my eyes lit up. My namesake island, covered with seabirds—it beckoned me. A year later, I would meet (in the Minnesota woods of all places) a photographer from Anchorage named Tom Soucek who would help me get there. Though the five-square-mile, privately-owned island in the Gulf of Alaska is uninhabited, the U.S. Fish and Wildlife Service conducts research on the nesting seabirds. Tom had visited the island before and put me in touch with Verena Gill, one of the chief researchers. When I called her, she could not believe that a guy named Middleton wanted to go to Middleton Island! Life can be stranger than fiction. Quite receptive to my request, she invited me to spend a week and even made a spare tent available to me.

In July 2000, a small plane dropped us off on Middleton Island and as I stepped onto the runway, I noticed an eagle nest not 100 yards away. That's what I call a good start. While driving to the campsite on an ATV, a bag of prized oranges, apples and bananas fell and were smashed by the tire into a gravel puree. How the tables can turn so quickly! With no creature comforts from home, I had finally heard the call of the wild, exploring and experiencing the elements by day and retreating into my cold nylon burrow by nightfall to eat my sardines. Had I become a seabird... this *Rhapsody in Blue* adventure was getting out of hand!

While the researchers were consumed by their many projects, I was free to roam the island by foot. The puffins, kittiwakes, and gulls were abundant and with lots of hard work, I was able to make some nice shots. Strolls on the rocky beaches also turned up lots of Black Oystercatchers and various sandpipers. My heart was really set on a great shot of a Bald Eagle nest. I anxiously awaited the return of the lead biologist, Scott, who had ventured out one day to a distant nest on a large beach boulder. As his ATV neared, I sensed something was off. His face and clothing were stained by clumps of dried blood. In good spirits, nonetheless, he related how an eagle had attacked him from behind as he approached the nest. Upon his scalp being raked by the eagle's needle-sharp

talons, he aborted his photo mission. My spirits sank, as I also intended to visit the island's only ground nest.

To go or not to go, that was the question that burned in my mind for the next 36 hours. My chief concern was not so much being attacked than if I was, there would be no one to help as the researchers were working at the other end of the island with no radio contact. Crummy weather the next day made my decision easy, but the next day was my last full day scheduled and I decided to go for it. I had not come this far to quit now, and I had never stepped down from a challenge on numerous other occasions since 1998. Armed with a spare bicycle helmet, I pedaled off to the foggy horizon cautiously optimistic.

Half of the adventure was just getting to the nest. Down a bumpy gravel road on a Brady Bunch vintage bicycle with a broken seat, a 30-pound backpack nestled between the rusted handlebars. Then hike down and up a ravine. And then a mile hike across Fern Gully, a maze of steep bumps of soil rendered invisible by a jungle of chest-high ferns. Twice I fell, my feet sliding down the slippery slopes of the tussocks, the heavy backpack throwing off my balance. After expressing some pretty salty language, I got back up, ruffled my feathers and forged on, finally making it to the edge of the cliff, where I was told I would be able to see the nest on the beach.

Peering over the vast beach—perhaps 200 yards wide and 600 yards long—I was looking down on a sea of boulders. Did I take a wrong turn in Fern Gully? Perplexed as to my next move, I took delight in the first blue sky I had seen in five days. Puffins were whizzing by, some with fish in their bill, so I tried for flight shots. Later, I saw an eagle fly by, then another and I scoured the beach again. Ah hah! There it was, a large rock covered with sticks and two brown specs on it. Scampering down the cliff, I approached the nest, double and triple checking that my helmet had not fallen off. To my surprise, the eagles never flew too close, preferring to monitor the situation from their clifftop roost.

I was able to make some nice images of the two large chicks from the ground, but the shoot felt incomplete. It dawned on me that I really needed to be in the nest, but the eight-foot boulder had smooth vertical walls with no cracks for footing. I then realized that I could stack driftwood from the beach at the base of the rocks, so I did. Finally, I grabbed onto a

large securely woven stick in the nest and hoisted myself up— I was perched with eagles. Fully expecting the adults to attack at this point, they just sat on the cliff and watched. The chicks also showed no signs of alarm, though I can only imagine what they were thinking! I even did a self-portrait with my new friends (p. 238). This is my favorite *Rhapsody in Blue* moment. This is my Mt. Everest, all eight feet of it.

Only one experience would eclipse the glory of sitting with eagles. In December 2000, I journeyed to Isla Isabela off the Mexican Coast. Accomplished nature photographer Tim Fitzharris described his visit to Isabela in *Nature Photography Hotspots*, and it sounded like heaven. Our guide was a fisherman and birder from the seaside town of San Blas, halfway down Mexico's Pacific Coast. We met Armando in town and stocked up on fruits and vegetables at a local market. We loaded up his 20-foot open-cabin fishing boat and headed off for the 43-mile trip. How odd it must have looked to the locals as we carried large suitcases in knee-high water to his anchored boat. Little did we know that the 2 1/2 hour trip would take 10 hours. The wind picked up so we took shelter behind a sea stack 100 feet tall where seabirds rested.

By sunset, the waves were still choppy, but I decided to make a run for it—hoping that the wind would die. As it turned out, the seas never calmed. To make matters worse, we were headed straight into the wind for a four-hour ballbuster. On a brighter note, the stars were exquisite that night, and we noticed lights in the sky moving in ways that neither celestial bodies nor human aircraft typically do. Armando informed us that this area was a hotbed for UFO activity, and we were being watched. At one point, my travelling companion, Jessica, and I burst out in laughter at the absurdity of the whole situation. Shortly before midnight, we finally arrived in pitch-blackness.

Sleeping on the boat, we awoke to Paradise—jagged emerald-green mountains, turquoise waters, birds filling the sky, and a beach lined with fisherman's huts like a South Pacific movie set. The next four days were nothing short of bliss. Most of the birds were quite tame and could be approached at very close range, none more so than the ground-nesting Brown and Blue-footed Boobies. Many of the Brown Boobies had downy white chicks. One adult stuck his face in my lens (pp. 10-11) as I did a wide angle scenic shot. The Blue-footed Boobies are famous for their rather goofy courtship dance, but I was particularly taken by their dramatic landings, feet flared straight out to break the wind. Hundreds of Magnificent Frigatebirds also call Isabela home, nesting in bushes and short trees. I was endlessly entertained by the male's flamboyant inflatable red pouch, deployed when in high spirits.

I would be remiss if I did not say a few words about Maryland, my home and host for the nation's largest and most celebrated estuary, the Chesapeake Bay. For every day spent in some exotic location, I probably spent three shooting virtually in my own backyard. Many of Rhapsody's images are from Maryland. As a child growing up in Baltimore, I

have early memories of Osprey nesting on channel markers, cornfields full of Canada Geese, and Great Blue Heron reigning tall in their watery domain. While preparing *Maryland's Great Outdoors* from 1993 to 1996, I really began to appreciate our amazingly diverse habitats, plants, and animals. Our charismatic waterbird species especially enthralled me.

Though the diversity of Maryland waterbirds is impressive, there are no premier venues for photography that would compare to Bosque del Apache, Estero Lagoon, Bolsa Chica, or Cape May. Maryland birds are not generally acclimated to hordes of photographers seeking portraits; getting close can be a problem. Fortunately, I had been building a network of contacts who would tip me off on special locations. My two favorite spots in Maryland were discovered in this manner.

My favorite local spot is the Patterson Park Boat Lake in Baltimore City; I refer to it as the "Miracle Pond." In the fall of 1999, I received a fateful call from a dear friend, Gerda Deterer, who runs Wildlife Rescue in Central Maryland. Aware of my passion for bird photography, Gerda informed me that she had just seen Wood Ducks in this urban park. The boat lake was regarded by many as an eyesore, its fence and sidewalks in disrepair, overrun by cattails, and repository for bottles and snack wrappers. Nonetheless, as my inventory of wild woodie shots was miniscule, I eagerly made the 10-minute jaunt from my downtown rowhouse. Sure enough, a half dozen drakes and hens were spotted among the flotilla of Mallards. The next day, I returned with camera gear and a bag of corn. To my delight, the woodies would accept handouts. Day after day, season after season, I was drawn to the pond, and before I knew it, two years and 1200 rolls of film had passed. I was able to document many aspects of their life cycle, including woodies perched in trees. A surprising 20 species used the lake to varying degrees. The net result of all of this a new book, *The Miracle Pond*, that is in the works.

Another wonderful spot was revealed to me when a lovely lady by the name of Lisa Glorioso contacted me in 1998 about doing a slide show for her camera club. The waterbird project came up, and she invited me down to check out the Tundra Swans and bay ducks that she and her husband, Bryan, were feeding on their creek in Severna Park. When corn was thrown out, dozens of the giant white visitors from the North glided in while the ducks—Canvasback, Redhead, and Lesser Scalp—rained in like a hail of gunfire. This place was magic. I made several visits that winter of 1998, drawn to the dramatic sparring of the swans, with loud honks, intimidating open-wing posturing, and neck-biting. Despite the cold, I grew quite fond of my ring-side seat on the Chesapeake Bay.

I was shocked to learn of Lisa's sudden passing, a true gem of a human being with a bright light radiating from her core. Within days of that sad phone call, I was stunned to look through my living room window and see a Sharp-shinned Hawk, not a typical sight in downtown Baltimore. I sensed Lisa's spirit, her passion for birds, and the inter-connectedness that we all share. Four years later, while working on this very piece, I photographed an adult sharpie perched in a neighbor's tree perhaps 30 feet from the prior sighting. The connection endures, as does Lisa's spirit.

Getting back to the big picture... by December 2001, I sensed that the shooting of *Rhapsody in Blue* was drawing to a close. I had just gotten the last shot on my wish list... wild Hooded Mergansers at Druid Hill Park in Baltimore City. Besides, I was exhausted, broke and my slide binders were now overflowing into my guest shower. Nearly four years after that poor muskrat met his match in a Great Blue Heron, I was spent. I had taken thirty major trips outside of the Mid-Atlantic region. Of the approximately 240 species of breeding North American waterbirds, I had photographed 185 in the wild, traveled an estimated 90,000 miles, shot 195,000 slides, and spent more money than I care to admit. It was time to make a book.

While shooting *Rhapsody in Blue*, I came to realize that something big in my life was unfolding. What started out as an ambitious photographer searching for beautiful birds evolved into a discovery of joy, peace and truth. Ego fuelled my fire in the beginning, but somewhere along the way the "me" part of it lost significance. I knew that I had a divine partner in the project who made it all possible. There were just too many times when dreamed-up images in my mind would actually happen on film for it to be a case of good luck, a winning streak, or mind over matter. No longer compelled to make the shot at any cost, I was just glad to have such a wonderful job, to be able to experience such natural beauty, to be able to wake up each morning with a smile on my face. I had finally acknowledged the spirit of God working in me, a partner who always keeps a promise.

Just as I was hooking into my own spirit, I was recognizing that my quarry had a spirit deserving of respect, as does all life. I am still amazed at the Wood Ducks of Patterson Park. Wood Ducks are a shy lot, but God provided a handful of individuals that could be viewed close-up as they lived their lives at the Miracle Pond. I started to recognize individual birds by subtle markings and curious personality traits. Some were definitely more comfortable with me than others. I communicated all of the different kinds of shots that I wanted, and the birds revealed these moments over an extended period of time. Clearly a divine authority arranged the schedule of these moments. For every reason that a person would have a soul, so too must a wild creature. Pondering such thoughts,

I developed a whole new respect and love for all living beings. Today, I will capture a wayward house fly and release it outside; there is no compulsion to swat it to death. I truly believe as I developed a sense of respect for all life, the animals revealed themselves to me in special ways that before were not available to me. I do not feel a sense of entitlement, but I willingly accept these blessings as a gift and symbol of God's amazing grace and love for us as we struggle to make sense of this life and find a purpose that brings joy to our hearts and peace of mind.

Looking back at my long list of concerns, I am still amazed at how each of them was addressed. First and foremost, how would I find and successfully photograph all 150 target species? As it turned out, with a lot of help, a parade of angels who would tip me off to key locations. What a generous and loving God. Concerning finances, my photography business of stock and assignment work generated just enough income to pay for all the film, airfare, lodging and guide fees. When things got tight, I could count on the phone ringing with a new project. This great adventure also challenged me physically like never before. Despite a life-long struggle with asthma, I forged on with each opportunity, gradually building up my strength and endurance. Other concerns like losing equipment checked through suitcases, damaged film, and bad weather also weighed on my mind, but I decided to no longer worry my life away. As with everything else, I just had faith that somehow it would all work out and forged ahead.

I would like to share one last story about faith that really encapsulates the spirit of this life-altering project. I traveled to Barrow, Alaska (inside the Arctic Circle) in June of 2000 in search of the King Eider duck. I had only "discovered" this duck two years prior in a field guide, blown away by its gaudy colors. I could have photographed one in a zoo and saved a lot of time and money, but I felt compelled to see it on its own terms, like all of the birds in this collection. Several days into the trip, no King Eider had been seen in Barrow, where my friend, Tom Soucek, had photographed them at close range the year prior. Despite nice looks at several arctic nesters, I desperately wanted the king, and losing all hope, I changed our flight plans to leave early. The second to last day, Rinker and I were parked by the beach, observing the sea ice, when a van of birdwatchers stopped by to shoot the breeze. I was stunned to hear the guide say that they had just seen a King Eider down the road in a pond near a maintenance building. We zoomed down the road, and there he was, swimming in all his glory in a small pool surrounded by ice. The beautiful drake allowed us to approach within twenty feet, an impossible request for a wild duck not acclimated to people. That day, and the next I took nearly thirty rolls of him. At one point, he swam within the minimum focus range of the lens, maybe six feet away. Tipping up to feed in the shallow water, he made himself truly vulnerable; he must have sensed that we meant him no harm. For an open-ocean duck that most likely had never seen people before, this was mind-boggling. Just when I had given up hope, I was blessed with a most amazing miracle.

The grace of God kept pouring into my life, well beyond the birds I treasured. Seeking a new relationship in the fall of 2000, I put my written request in a wine bottle, launched in Baltimore from Fort McHenry, birthplace of our National Anthem. In December, I received a phone call from an old friend who had someone for me to meet by the name of Kristie Edwards. We have shared seven enlightening years together, growing, healing and celebrating life. Kristie introduced me to Mountain Christian Church in Joppa, Maryland. Reluctantly, I agreed to visit once. In exchange, Kristie faced her fear of flying by traveling to St. Augustine with me to photograph birds. I was pleasantly surprised by my first visit and returned. Upon absorbing several compelling sermons, by Senior Pastor Ben Cachiaras, I could no longer reject the truth before my eyes, ears and heart. In May 2001, I accepted Christ as my personal Savior and Lord, and I chose to express my faith in symbolic baptism. Since that time, I have developed a sense of inner peace and calm that gets me through difficult times. I cannot fathom returning to my old way of life, living with no compass while chasing an illusionary happiness filled with stuff beyond my control. I am eternally grateful for being guided on this path overflowing with joy, wonder, community and a sense of purpose.

I hope that these photographs of North American's wondrous waterbirds help you grow in your appreciation of nature's many gifts. I feel truly blessed to be given the opportunity to witness and share with you these telling moments. Though these images point to a vibrant and abundant community of North American waterbirds, many species and habitats are in peril. There are numerous actions that we as individuals can take to promote better stewardship of our natural heritage. Support conservation orginizations like the National Audubon Society, The Nature Conservancy and World Wildlife Fund, to name a few. I encourage all of you to make a conscious decision to get involved and make a difference, so future generations can also experience such wild beauty and marvel at the genius design of Creation.

I also hope that this story inspires you to release your fears and inhibitions and jump into the flow of life. Live each day with intention, integrity, and joy. *Rhapsody in Blue* is ultimately a celebration of life. Chase your dreams with the wild abandon of a plunging pelican! Persistence, patience and confidence will yield fruit in abundance.

CHAPTER ONE
The Portait Gallery

One has only to consider the life force packed tight into that puff of feathers to lay the mind wide open to the mysteries—the order of things, the why and the beginning. As we contemplate that sanderling, there by the shining sea, one question leads inevitably to another, and all questions come full circle to the questioner, paused momentarily in his own journey under the sun and sky.

—Peter Mattiessen

The Long and the Short of it

The multiple forms, plumages and behaviors of shorebirds make them both a challenge and a joy to observe. The smallest sandpipers, known as "peeps," can appear nearly identical at a distance. Pictured here are the Least Sandpiper (*below right*) and Semipalmated Sandpiper (*below left*). Equally diminutive is the endangered Piping Plover (*above*), yet it is readily identifiable in breeding plumage. Towering over the sparrow-sized peeps on delicate red legs is the Black-necked Stilt (*left*). Standing 15 inches tall, its exaggerated profile appears somewhat improbable, if not whimsical. Even the tallest shorebird is dwarfed by the statuesque Wood Stork (*following pages*), a wading bird of southern swamps. Reptilian neck scales mark the left-hand bird as an adult, while the juvenile sports a feathered coiffe.

Captain Hook

The spirit of the pirate is alive and well on the high seas. Few birds look the part more convincingly than the Double-crested Cormorant *(above)* and Magnificent Frigatebird *(left)*. A hooked bill is the trademark of a fisherman—cormorants chase down fish underwater while frigatebirds pluck fish on the fly. Yet stealing a meal works well too, especially for the latter seaman. The male cormorant's jet-black body only accentuates his fancy crested head with an orange facemask, turquoise eyes, and powder-blue mouth. This handsome frigatebird is a juvenile male; he will not don the black suit until four or five years old.

The Coast Guard

Coastal marine waters host a great variety of seabirds, each uniquely designed to exploit various food sources. A blood-red bill is the signature of the Heermann's Gull (*left*), denizen of the lower Pacific Coast. Like other gulls it scavenges for remains and dips for live prey, but it is also a confirmed pirate, raiding pelicans, boobies, and, not surprisingly, others of its tribe. The streamlined Royal Tern (*below*) is a plunge-diver, snatching fish, squid, and shrimp that venture precariously close to the surface. The Tufted Puffin (*right*) is one of North America's three beloved species of "sea parrots," as they are affectionately known. It dives deep in cooler North Pacific waters in hot pursuit of small schooling fish. The stout bill, capable of gripping several fish at a time, is brightly colored only during the breeding season.

$\mathcal{T}$he Dapper Drake

Admired the world over for their bold patterns and flashy colors, male ducks have inspired a whole subculture, symbolized by such icons as decoys, embroidered clothing and the ever-popular Labrador Retriever. In all but a few of North America's nearly three dozen nesting species, the drake's plumage is dashing in comparison to the subdued hen. Posing for the infrequent portrait (wild ducks are wary) are two divers, the Long-tailed Duck (*right*) and King Eider (*above*), and a dabbler, the Blue-winged Teal (*below*). The drake's good looks serve him well when competing for mating rights with unpaired hens. Unlike swans and geese, which pair for life, ducks seek out new partners each spring, and thus courtship rituals play a greater role in their nesting season. Once eggs are laid, the spirited drakes depart and the hen will raise her brood alone.

The Humble Hen

Dressed in cryptic browns and grays, female ducks are not as readily identifiable as their showy male companions. The drab plumage deflects any unwanted attention while incubating eggs, typically on a ground nest, and when escorting ducklings through predator-laden wetlands. The four species represented here are the Ring-necked Duck (*right*), Northern Pintail (*lower right*), American Wigeon (*lower left*), and Green-winged Teal (*below*). The iridescent green swatch, called the "speculum," on this teal's secondary feathers is normally tucked in while resting. A common feature of both sexes of various dabbling ducks, the speculum's lustrous color is not due to pigmentation but rather the refraction of light striking minute feather structures.

Seeing Red

Kindred spirits, loons and grebes have fished the world's oceans and lakes for untold millenia. Five species of loon, including the Pacific Loon (*left*) and seven grebe varieties–this is a Western Grebe (*right*)–call North America home. Supremely adapted to life in the water, they are awkward on land and reluctant fliers. Nests are constructed at the water's edge, offering a quick underwater escape when necessary. The practice of ferrying young on their back endears both families to naturalists the world over. These two birds did not hatch out to see the world through a ruby lens, but rather acquired the vivid color as a rite of passage. Eye color can also vary according to the sexual cycle in certain species of bird.

The Vise Squad

The handsome Northern Harrier, also known as the "Marsh Hawk," is one of several birds of prey that live in intimate association with North American wetlands. Its needle-sharp talons are familiar to many that stir beneath—grasshoppers, frogs, voles and sparrows, to name a few. Adult harriers feature lemon-yellow eyes and a white rump patch, best viewed in flight, but it is the gray male (*above*) that is most awe-inspiring. Identifying a brown harrier (*left*) as a female or juvenile male can be difficult, especially in the morning mist. The regal Bald Eagle (*following pages*) is commonly viewed across much of North America, thanks to a heralded comeback from the brink of extinction once pesticides linked to poor reproduction were banned in 1972. The juvenile birds on the right will not command a white head and tail until the fourth or fifth year, when a life partner is sought. In excess of 100,000 Bald Eagles grace the continent, the vast majority in Alaska and Canada.

Feathered Swords

A wading bird's pride and joy is its tapered, dagger-like bill that pierces or pinches live prey. The Great Blue Heron (*above & right*) makes a presence throughout the lower 48 states into Canada and southern Alaska. Its huge bill is employed to dispatch a great variety of critters, including birds, snakes and small mammals. In south Florida, especially the Keys, one may encounter a splendid white-phase bird (*right*). This tall wader is easily confused with the ubiquitous Great Egret (*left*) except for its pinkish legs; the Great Egret always has black legs. The Cattle Egret (*previous pages, left*) is another splendid white egret, especially during the breeding season. Curiously, it is an immigrant from Africa (via South America) that colonized the New World without human intervention, reaching the United States in the 1950s. The splendid Tricolored Heron, (*previous pages, right*) a medium-sized wader, can be seen in coastal states from New England to Texas. This individual illustrates the dramatic makeover some herons experience during peak courtship.

*D*ouble Vision

Matching wardrobes make distinguishing the sexes quite a challenge with many kinds of waterbirds. This close-up view of Mute Swans (*right*) illustrates the male's more prominent black knob above the bill. He also stands a bit taller than his life-long mate. The White-cheeked Pintail (*above*) of the Bahamas and the West Indies is an odd duck in that the sexes have similar coloring. A brilliant green speculum is concealed in this resting posture. Noted for its crimson forehead shield, the Common Moorhen (*below*) is an easily recognized resident of southern ponds and marshes. Just as comfortable on land as water, it walks chicken-like on yellowish-green legs.

Between the Lines

Reclusive by nature, rails and bitterns live highly secretive lives, providing steadfast birders only an occasional glimpse. Despite its impressive size, the American Bittern (*below*) shies away from open space, preferring to lurk amidst tall grasses and reeds. The much smaller Least Bittern (*right*) is light enough to traverse the marsh without wetting its feet, gripping sturdy reeds with dexterous toes. When alarmed, both species attempt a disappearing act by freezing, neck and bill elongated skyward to expose vertical stripes that mimic their reedy surroundings. The cryptic California Clapper Rail (*lower right*) is a phantom of the salt marsh, melding into its environs at the slightest suspicion. Also found in the dense vegetation are the Purple Gallinule (*following pages, right*) of sub-tropical swamps and marshes, and the Northern Jacana (*following pages, left*) of Mexico and south Texas. Although brightly colored, these lily-hoppers can be elusive, feeding on the move through tangles of emergent plants.

Mister Personality

Beyond good looks, many a bird is fabled for curious behaviors and traits. With bold rattling cries, the Belted Kingfisher (*right*) proclaims fishing rights to lakes and streams across the continent. Any approach or unwelcome glance will send this notoriously wary bird fleeing. Do not let the bold posturing of a Pied-billed Grebe (*below*) fool you; it is also a reclusive bird. When alarmed, it disappears under the surface and hides in reeds undetected with only its bill breaking the surface. The Limpkin (*left*), so-named for its crippled gate, is infamous for loud calls after the sun sets. Plovers (*following pages, left*) include the Pacific Golden-Plover (*top*) and Wilson's Plover (*bottom*); they are famous for their broken-wing nest distraction displays. These plump beachcombers have very short bills by shorebird standards, hunting by sight rather than probing for hidden edibles. Phalaropes (*following pages, right*) are equally fascinating subjects; pictured here are the Red Phalarope (*bottom*) and Wilson's Phalarope (*top*). Sex roles are reversed in these most unusual shorebirds; the less attractive male is responsible for tending eggs and young.

Flights of Fancy

"...and the moment you doubt whether you can fly, you cease to be able to do it. The reason birds can fly and we can't is simply that they have perfect faith, for to have faith is to have wings."

—Sir James Matthew Barrie

*G*one with the Wind

Diverse seabirds cruise the oceans in a never-ending search for nourishment. Wing design reveals much about a bird's livelihood. The elongated, narrow wings of certain pelagic birds like the Northern Gannet (*far left*) and Northern Fulmar (*left and right*) facilitate long periods of gliding in their northern windy haunts. Thus energy reserves are conserved while searching for scattered feeding opportunities. The Tufted Puffin (*above center*) is not a glider; like other auks, it must flap its stubby wings constantly to stay airborne in labored flight. However, the undersized wings make excellent flippers underwater when schools of fish are pursued. The Arctic Tern (*below*) sports a forked tail, which assists in the hover-and-dive swooping sequence used in fishing. It is a long-distance champion, migrating upwards of 10,000 miles between the Poles.

J et Lag

The long, pointed wings of shorebirds produce strong, dynamic flight, necessitated by a penchant for long migrations and for escaping the winged terror that is an attacking falcon. Tundra breeders like the Ruddy Turnstone (*above*) are among the international jet-set, passing through many countries over a lifetime. Turnstones from North America's arctic fringe disperse in late summer to Australia, New Zealand, Hawaii, South America, and Europe, burning a significant portion of their body weight to fuel epic non-stop flights over water. Larger species like the Willet (*left*) and Marbled Godwit (*top*) tend to be interstate travelers, with a few exceptions, moving between interior grasslands for nesting and coastal beaches and mudflats for wintering. Highly sociable, shorebirds travel in flocks, none more familiar than the Sanderling (*following pages*), another champion globetrotter.

Flight School

Takeoffs and landings are moments of high drama as birds transition between the realms of free ethereal spirits and gravity-bound creatures. These ducks gracefully demonstrate such tactical maneuvers—an acquired skill, as many a fledgling with a bruised ego can attest. The rising sun silhouettes a Northern Pintail (*left*) springing into flight, dabbling-duck fashion, on a western lake. Diving ducks like the Lesser Scaup (*above and below*) typically taxi across the water, sprinting forward on legs anchored towards the stern. Such an alignment makes ground landings ill-advised and they are avoided at all cost. This drake is pictured at the moment of touch-down, splashing across the surface until forward momentum is halted while a hen sprints across the surface to generate lift.

*R*ush Hour

Beginning with dawn's first light, birds are on the move, dispersing from secure nighttime roosts to prime feeding areas. Having burned precious calories throughout the night to stay warm, energy stores must be replenished. These Sandhill Cranes and Snow Geese (*below*) have set their sights on agricultural fields where refuse from the harvest awaits. The characteristic flight formation of geese and others are believed to be a function of the improved aerodynamics when a trailing bird catches an updraft from a forward member of the flock. A trio of Double-crested Cormorants (*lower left*) motor to their favorite fishing hole at the crack of dawn. Soft twilight renders an impressionistic view of a Black Skimmer flock alighting (*left*). Acute night vision in this most unusual bird permits feeding when their competitors are fast asleep.

J urassic Park

The teradactyl silhouette of wheeling pelicans is a resonating, primal symbol that recalls an age when dinosaurs ruled the land and sky. Considering their tremendous bulk, pelicans are surprisingly agile on the wing. These Brown Pelicans (*left and right*) are springing into flight like a puddle duck, kicking their large webbed feet simultaneously and pumping their massive wings for vertical thrust. Strong fliers, the Brown Pelican has a wing span upwards of seven feet, while its larger cousin, the American White Pelican (*above*) measures nearly ten feet. Pelicans often travel in groups low over water, like this quartet of American White Pelicans at a Rocky Mountain lake. The standard formation is a tapered line of birds evenly spaced, wingbeats asynchronous as followers keep pace with the next in line.

*W*hite *Flight*

Having no particular need for speed, wading birds seem to flutter like apparitions across wetlands, gentle spirits in a workaholic world. The broad wings of these birds—Snowy Egret (*above*), Great Egret (*left*) and While Ibis (*top left*)—must be flapped continuously to maintain sufficient lift at their relatively slow speeds of travel. Over the course of a day, wading birds typically move short distances from feeding to roosting spots, keeping their time aloft to a minimum. Before waterways freeze up on the continent's northern fringe, wading birds migrate hundreds of miles to the south where ice cannot form to separate them from their slippery prey. The exception to this rule is the Great Blue Heron, who is not averse to snow on his back, but still requires partial open water for hunting.

$\mathcal{B}$ay Watch

Nimble on the wing, gulls rely on their agility and tenacity to sustain their opportunistic feeding habits. The Bonaparte's Gull (*above*), pictured here in winter plumage, earns a respectable living dipping for minnows and the like. This small, tree-nesting gull also has a taste for insects, sometimes taken in the air. The distinctive Heermann's Gull (*top left*) is a master of tight turns and quick climbs, maneuvers sometimes employed to heist another bird's meal, yet it is also a skilled fisherman. One only needs to watch the commonplace Ring-billed Gull (*top right*) fight over handouts at the beach to appreciate the aerial supremacy of gulls. Large gulls like the Western Gull (*right*) feature broader wings and reduced quickness, not so much a problem when pursuing sedentary items like eggs, sea urchins and mussels, a few favorites.

Lost in Paradise

North America's subtropical regions play host to extravagant winged jewels, enticing birders thousands of miles from home with the prospect of a thrilling fly-by. The Greater Flamingo (*above*) is a real straight arrow on the wing. Large breeding colonies are scattered in Mexico and the Caribbean, but sightings of wild birds are consistent in the Florida Keys along with escaped captive birds in South Florida. On a lush tropical island off Mexico's Pacific coast, a Blue-footed Booby (*left*) braces for a crash landing on a craggy cliff where a new generation of boobies are nurtured. Crevices on those same cliffs attract another beauty, the Red-billed Tropicbird (*below*), a cavity nester that features whimsical tail streamers. This dorsal view shows the adult's barred back, a bird easily confused with the similarly profiled White-tailed Tropicbird.

$\mathcal{S}$ wan Lake

For the heavy-bodied swan, becoming airborne requires a long stretch of open water to tread vigorously on massive webbed feet. This Mute Swan (*below*) makes quite a splash taxing down a runway on the Chesapeake Bay, where they have established a stronghold upon escaping from captivity a few decades ago. The native Tundra Swan (*left*) is more gregarious than its orange-billed, Old World cousin. During migration, it travels in large flocks, which break up into smaller family groups on their wintering grounds. Tipping the scales at thirty pounds, the colossal Trumpeter Swan (*following pages*) boasts a wing span of eight feet, the largest of North America's waterfowl. This adult and fledgling below are depicted during flight lessons around their natal lake in Minnesota, a former Midwest territory where these rare birds have been re-introduced.

Tunnel Vision

North America's waterways represent a grand banquet for those scouring from above with binocular vision. The forward-facing eyes of predatory birds can discern detail many times greater than a human eye. Inexperienced birdwatchers may confuse our two fishing raptors, similar in size and profile from a distance. A close fly-by reveals marked differences; the Bald Eagle's (*following pages*) dark underside is very distinct from the Osprey's (*left*) barred feathers and white belly. In addition, the leading edge of an eagle's wing is straight, that of a fish hawk bent at the elbow. The stunning Swallow-tailed Kite (*below*), a buoyant acrobat, hunts swamps and bayous of the Deep South. Prey such as tree frogs, snakes, lizards, and insects are not taken directly from the water but snagged on the fly and occasionally eaten in mid-air. However, the Snail Kite (*above*) most certainly dunks its talons when plucking apple snails from lakes. Female Snail Kites are mottled brown, unlike the dashing slate-blue male.

*D*ucks Unlimited

Despite a high ratio of body weight to wing surface area (wing loading), ducks are superlative fliers. Rapid wing beats powered by strong pectoral muscles make them the speed demons of waterfowl. A few individuals have been clocked at 70 mph, but normally cruise at much slower speeds when unhurried. Starring in a hunter's dream are a Black-bellied Whistling Duck (*left*), Canvasback (*right*), Mallard (*upper right*) and Bufflehead (*above*). Decades of reckless hunting and habitat degradation have brought a number of duck populations down from historic levels, but careful censusing and management practices ensure that most species are stable from year to year. Natural predators claim their fair share, of course; perhaps there is one less Mallard or Snow Goose (*following pages*) launching into flight at a refuge known for its crafty coyotes.

Three Square Meals

The sight of any free animal going about its business undisturbed, seeking its food, or looking after its young, or mixing in the company of its kind, all the time being exactly what it ought to be and can be—what a strange pleasure it gives us! ...there is only one mendacious being in the world and that is man. Every other is true and sincere, and makes no attempt to conceal what it is expressing its feelings just as they are.

—Arthur Schopenhauer

Close Encounters

One can only speculate as to the thoughts that may cross the minds of our animal friends, especially in times of high drama. This inquisitive Western Gull (*above*) is sharing a moment with an elephant seal pup on the California coast. Sandwiched by two large females, the pup is in no danger; it is the placenta of newborns that draws gull concentrations each winter to these traditional birthing areas. This pup's afterbirth was devoured by two dozen gulls within minutes of its arrival. Across the continent a Herring Gull (*right*) issues a death sentence to a protesting calico crab fished from the surf on a New Jersey beach. Seconds later the stalemate was broken as the gull disarmed the crustacean with its strong bill.

On the Rocks

Chronic workaholics, shorebirds feed throughout the day to meet the energy demands of a frenetic lifestyle. On a good day a third of their body weight in food may be consumed. Rocky coastlines and jetties are inviting habitats that offer a bevy of treats—barnacles, limpets,

amphipods, crabs, mollusks, worms and insects. Among the specialists drawn to the splash zone are the Ruddy Turnstone (*above*), Black Turnstone (*center left*), Spotted Sandpiper (*lower left*) and Purple Sandpiper (*upper left*). Long toes help to grip the slippery rocks while foraging. The turnstones are especially entertaining when flipping rocks, shells, and seaweed to uncover hidden morsels. Come springtime they will migrate inland and feed on an entirely different host of organisms at their breeding grounds. A high tide of breeding horseshoe crabs (*following pages*) transforms a sandy beach along the Delaware Bay. These Short-billed Dowitchers and other shorebirds feast on the tiny crab eggs to fuel the last leg of their spring migration to the Canadian tundra.

Rich Man, Poor Man

When it comes to animals having to make do in a world of limited resources, honor is not a factor for consideration. Stealing food is part of the natural order and some have perfected it into an art form. Never one to miss a golden opportunity, a Laughing Gull (*below*) has snatched fish remains from the pelican's mouth. The gull launched its brazen attack while perched on the pelican's head. This Magnificent Frigatebird (*bottom left*) maneuvers its wings and tail to close the gap on its target, the Blue-footed Booby. Either the booby dives for cover, as frigatebirds do not swim, or a fish is regurgitated for the toll collector. The Snowy Egret (*top right*) is an excellent fisherman, but he is also an opportunist; what escapes the probing forceps of a neighboring White Ibis may end up on the short end of the egret's black spear.

The Butcher's Block

Few scenes in the avian world are more compelling than an attacking eagle on the mark. With flared talons, the trap is set (*left*) as the huge raptor skims over the surface to lunge for a fish. The wings remain dry (unlike an Osprey) as the vise tightens on the extracted fish (*top left*). Larger fish must be carefully assessed as the bird could be pulled under once its hooks are anchored in the flesh. Though glorious when taking prey on the fly, eagles are just as apt to scavenge. They will not hesitate to capitalize on easy meals such as a windfall of discarded salmon scraps (*above*). Powerful beaks make quick work of the meat as it is pulled off the skeleton. Territorial during the nesting season, Bald Eagles congregate during the winter when concentrated food sources become available, most notably late-season salmon runs in Alaska.

Lightning Strikes

To secure a meal, herons stab at fish, frogs, tadpoles and others with a blistering jab, either spearing or pinching their hapless prey. Due to the relatively short legs and reclusive nature of our two smallest waders— the Green Heron (*this page*) and Least Bittern (*left*)—they frequently hunt from reeds and branches overlooking water. A normal resting posture would suggest a short neck, but such is not the case as they extend to amazing lengths to deploy the spring-loaded harpoon. These hunters practice the virtue of patience, waiting motionless for long periods until a tempting target passes within range.

$\mathcal{H}$oly Mackerel

Waders like this Reddish Egret (*right*) make fast work of minnows, but occasionally they target larger prey. With considerable effort, this Great Blue Heron (*left*) manages to swallow the huge fish. After a prolonged battle with a sand-bar shark, this Great Black-backed Gull (*above*) flew off with its ingested prize. Not unlike a snake, the mouth and esophagus are highly expandable. So as not to overload the digestive system, pre-packaged meals like a large fish can be stored in the crop, a flexible sack at the base of the throat that empties into the stomach. Lacking the cutlery of a raptor to tear off bits of meat, waders and seabirds can thus capitalize on a nutrition windfall. Of course, there are limits to this adaptation as a Great Blue Heron (*following pages*) is discovering; swallowing a large muskrat is really pushing the limits.

The Remains of the Day

If the avian world has a gourmand, it is the gull, as most dine on an extensive surf-and-turf menu. Lacking the talons, spears, forceps, and diving capabilities of its competitors, nature has gifted gulls with ingenuity and bravado. These scenes illustrate the versatile gull securing precious nutrients from fleeting opportunities. The afterbirth of a northern fur seal pup is highly nourishing, and a Glaucous Gull (*above*) is feasting like there is no tomorrow. This unsuspecting crab (*left*) was plucked from the receding surf by a Herring Gull, also shown picking at a bird's carcass (upper right) robbed from a nest. This hybrid Glacous-winged/Western Gull (*lower right*) has overestimated its abilities as a rigid starfish makes for a difficult meal to swallow.

The Big Gulp

Abundant fish in Florida's Everglades must run the daily gauntlet of numerous feathered fishermen attacking from all directions. The Anhinga (*top*) is an expert spearfisher. Buoyancy is regulated via internal air

sacs which allow this swamp denizen to submerge for hunting with hardly a ripple. When swimming, the Anhinga's sinuous neck may break the surface, hence the nickname "snakebird." The Double-crested Cormorant (*left*) sports a hooked bill, effective for grasping a fish caught in the vice. Upon surfacing, both species of divers must swallow their slippery catch head-first, so spiny fins fold inward against the birds' expandable throat. Fish must be tossed into the air until the correct angle of entry is obtained; some invariably slip away to live another day.

Dabblers and Divers

Waterfowl and other duck-like birds generally feed in one of two ways: dabbling for edibles at or near the water's surface or diving in pursuit of live prey and submerged vegetation. These summer Wood Duck drakes (*left*) live in a virtual salad bowl, nibbling on duckweed that covers their pond. Feeding from a perch is not customary; these birds are snacking during siesta. Like other geese, the Brandt (*above*) is a dabbler, stretching its long neck to reach eelgrass and other estuarine greens. When feeding in small groups, members alternate tipping-up to ensure that someone is always on the lookout for danger. The Lesser Scaup (*below*) is a classic diver; this duck has just extracted a huge mussel from the bottom. Canvasbacks (*following pages*) are also skilled divers, here mixing it up with Mallards and a few geese in a feeding frenzy.

Making a Splash

When not squabbling dockside over handouts of gutted fish scraps (*top*), Brown Pelicans feed as nature intended, by taking the plunge (*below*). Acrobatic dives target fish schooling near the surface. Upon impact the mouth opens to capture several litres of saltwater in the distended pouch. Flexible bones of the lower jaw bow out like a hoop to net fish stunned by the blow. Upon lifting and draining the pouch, anything that wiggles is swallowed. The American White Pelican (*left*) is not a plunge-diver, but instead scoops up fish while swimming, often working as a team to corral schooling baitfish in the shallows.

$\mathcal{P}$icky Eaters

With a hint of irony, two of North America's most elusive and sought-after waterbirds—the Snail Kite (*left*) and Limpkin (*above*)—owe their very existence to a most unglamorous snail. These birds are grasping apple snails, a large freshwater mollusk of the tropics that is their primary food source. Outside of Mexico and points south, Florida is the best place to see them. Neither stealth nor speed is necessary to catch the leisurely snail, but a precision tool is required to liberate the soft creature from its hard shell. Both the Snail Kite and Limpkin have highly specialized, albeit different bills to do just that. Apple snails are very sensitive to water quality. As Florida's wetlands have suffered decades of degradation, populations of this snail and these inspiring birds have declined markedly.

Sandtrap

Feeding shorebirds often adhere to the good neighbor policy. A variety of species may forage harmoniously on the same beach or mudflat, each working a niche largely defined by its bill length. There seems to be plenty to go around as a Willet (*near left*) and a Marbled Godwit (*far left*) probe a ball of seaweed for tiny edibles. The Long-billed Curlew (*below*) takes the prize for most outlandish bill; here it is grasping what appears to be a small mussel. Wading in shallow water has paid off handsomely for this Lesser Yellowlegs (*bottom*), holding an eel. It is unusual to see a shorebird with such a large catch. The dashing American Oystercatcher (*lower left*) has a taste for marine worms, cleansed by vigorous dunking to rid of excess grit.

Beauty and the Beast

Active feeding draws lots of unwanted attention from eyes high up on the food chain. This clear and present danger is amplified in lush southern swamps, where alligators (*above*) reign supreme. This fine specimen, photographed in Florida's Everglades, is brandishing his pearly whites to rival gators in the vicinity. When hunting it stalks almost fully submerged, eyes and snout just breaking the sur-

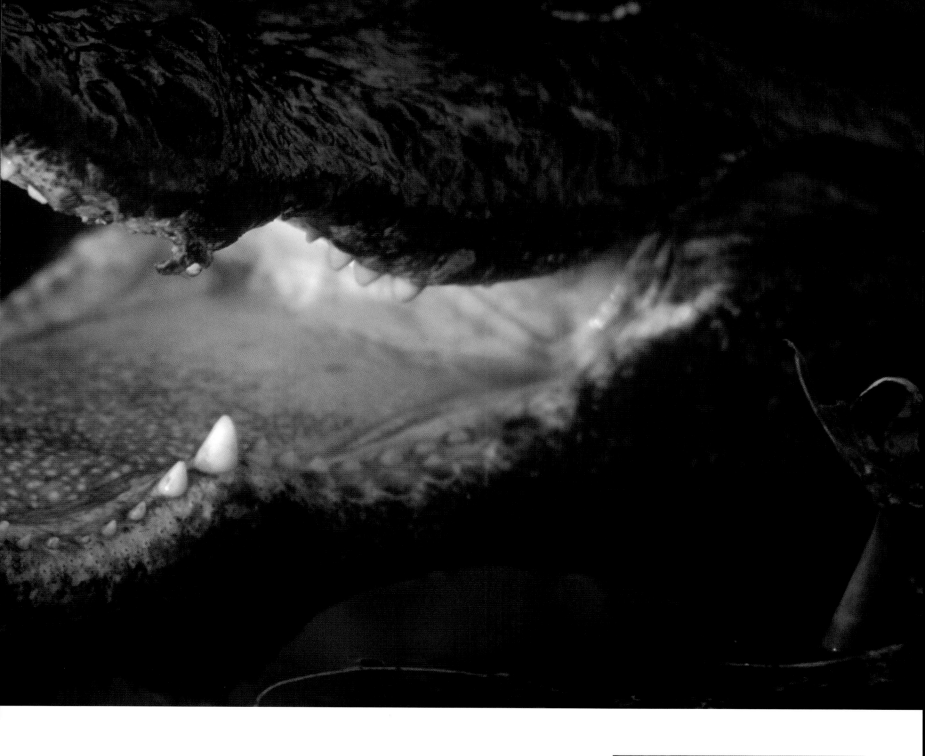

face. The Purple Gallinule (*top left*) is quite vulnerable to gator attacks when hopping across lily pads. Wading birds are another favorite; this young Snowy Egret nestling (*bottom left*) must not get jostled off its perch or its fate is sealed. Waterfowl that feed on farm fields must run the gauntlet of ambushing carnivores (*right*). Little remains of a goose that has lost the game to a pair of coyotes.

CHAPTER FOUR
The Daily Grind

We could live in a flat uninteresting world, one that had the bare minimum of gray ingredients to support life, one whose diversity was only enough to provide the minimum of existence. Instead, we live in a riotous explosion of diversity and beauty. We live in a world full of "useless" beauty, millions of species, and individuals of infinite variety, talents and abilities.

–Franky Schaeffer

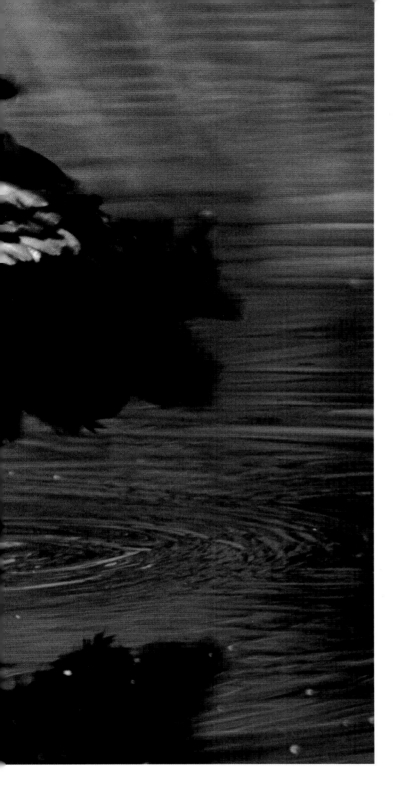

Bathing Beauties

Bird baths are not a matter of pleasure, but of survival. This daily maintenance routine is vital for good health. Various undesirable matter—dirt, lice, stale preen oil—accumulates in the plumage, and it must be rid to ensure a feather's peak performance. In the midst of a good soaking are a Redhead (*bottom*), Red Knot (*below*), Glossy Ibis (*left*) and Royal Tern (*lower left*). Not surprisingly, most waterbirds possess water-repellent feathers that provide insulation and buoyancy. Since water tends to bead-up on contact with feathers, birds must exert themselves with vigorous splashing and dunking to achieve adequate saturation and cleanliness. A thorough preening session follows to transform the ruffled bather into a perfectly contoured flying machine.

Drying Out

Spread-wind postures are characteristic of a handful of species especially fond of sunbathing. The Anhinga (*right*) and Double-crested Cormorant (*below*) hang their wings out to dry on a routine basis, usually after fishing. Their feathers are designed to be less water-repellent than other birds, thus decreasing buoyancy—not a bad thing when you chase down swimming fish for a living. Nonetheless, a wet wing is a liability should the need to fly arise. Exposing them to the sun helps to burn off excess moisture. Anhingas also posture to regulate their body temperatures, stretching their solar panels to soak up the sun at their back. This Great Blue Heron (*left*) has no need to dry out as its body stays dry when hunting. The curious pose is explained by the need to hold in check parasites that accumulate in the feathers. Exposure to bright sunlight prompts them to scatter, facilitating easier removal by the bill.

Keeping the Peace

Living in such close quarters as colonial waterbirds do, the potential for conflict is great and disputes are common. Intricate signals, whether vocal or visual, are well understood as tools to maintain family bonds and to indicate mounting tension when a violation has occurred. The highly animated Sandhill Crane (*left*) combines a booming voice (resonating from a 48-inch windpipe) with bold posturing like the spread-wing leap. The vociferous Tundra Swan (*above*) is an equally dramatic bird. When tensions boil over, a good bite to the neck is the only way to make a point. Gulls can also be quite quarrelsome; a Western Gull (*following pages*) is landing too close for the comfort of a protesting rival. Such disputes are often settled quickly, as it does not serve a bird well to drain

Up in Arms

Territory defense is a common chore during a bird's workday as strict boundaries must be enforced. An agitated Common Loon (*left*) appears to walk on water during the so-called "penguin dance." Violent splashing and visceral cries make it clear to others that their presence is not welcome. Any further approach usually results in an underwater retreat, disappearing for minutes before resurfacing a great distance away. The double-wing stretch of shorebirds like this American Oystercatcher (*right*) helps to warn neighbors that danger is imminent, none more alarming than a passing falcon. The feeding territory of this Reddish Egret (*below*) has just been invaded by another of its kind; this challenge is answered with a charge, plumes bristling with indignation.

$\mathcal{C}$old Feet

Survival in colder climates would not be possible if it were not for some amazing adaptations. These sparring Mallards (*above*), scratching Northern Shoveler (*below*) and resting Canada Goose (*right*) are rather comfortable during winter's icy grip. The heavily waterproofed plumage makes a great insulator, preserving body heat while keeping the cold air and water at bay. Tiny feathers on the body are compacted densely in order to trap air between them, warmed as energy reserves are burned off. An astonishing 7,500 feathers have been counted on a Wood Duck specimen, and 25,000 on a Tundra Swan. During cold spells, the legs and feet of waterfowl would seem to lose significant heat, but circulation to these extremities can be minimized. In addition, arteries and veins in the legs are aligned to exchange heat, warming up blood entering the body and cooling down blood headed to the feet, thus recycling heat into the body.

The 100-Yard Dash

Masters on the wing, birds are also capable of some pretty fancy footwork. This American Coot (*above*) is chasing off a rival, a drama that cantankerous coots may play out many times in the course of a day. Despite all of the wing flapping, it is rare to see them fly. The diminutive Sanderling (*lower left*) is arguably North America's most familiar shorebird, darting across the beach like a speed demon, always one step ahead of the surging surf. The rather languid Greater Flamingo (*upper left*) transforms into an athlete when taking flight, as it runs across the water on tiny webbed feet, accelerating and flapping to escape the pull of gravity. Also called the American Flamingo, this unmistakable bird may be seen in the wilds of south Florida, though some birds are undoubtedly escapees from captivity. Large colonies stage in Mexico, the Caribbean, and the Bahamas.

$\mathcal{T}$hird Watch

Aligned at different angles, these roosting ducks will have advance warning of any approaching predator. Foxes, coyotes and bobcats are a chief concern by land. Moreover, birds of prey patrol the sky as eternal enemies of the duck. Of course, ducks are also not particularly fond of people, with good reason. Rocky northern coastlines are the preferred winter haunts of the Harlequin Duck (*left*), more common on Pacific shores than Atlantic. The drake's fancy markings belie their blue-collar lifestyle, diving in turbulent mountain streams (summer) and churning surf for mollusks, crustaceans, and small fish. The Black-bellied Whistling Duck (*above*) is a very different animal. A gregarious tropical duck, it reaches its northern limits in Texas but strays well beyond. Male whistlers look identical to the females, and both participate in incubation (cavity nest) and rearing the young. Waterbirds tend to be highly social, forming large mixed flocks when resting and preening (*following pages*). Such congregations offer added comfort as there are numerous eyes to scout for trouble.

Vanity Fair

Daily grooming is crucial to maintaining the plumage's health and performance. The bill grabs each feather and smoothes it out to remove debris and to interlock the miniscule barbs that hold the structure together. Gathered from a small gland near the tail, preen oil is applied as a lubricant to ensure good strength, insulation, and waterproofing. This cast of yogis includes (*clockwise from right*) a Northern Pintail, Common Goldeneye, Great Egret, Anhinga, Short-billed Dowitcher, Mute Swan, and Green Heron.

Whiplash

To help maintain the flexibility of a pelican's prized pouch, a somewhat comical sequence of neck-stretching maneuvers is performed. Full extension of this California Brown Pelican's (*left*) fleshy crimson throat reveals a complex network of blood vessels normally hidden from view. To complete the stretch the lower jaw bows out and drops to invert the pouch against the neck. Caught in mid-stretch, this East Coast Brown Pelican (*right*) illustrates the lower bill's pliable nature. The whole routine is over in just a few seconds. The orange-billed American White Pelican (*above*) sports a matching gular sack that must also be exercised at regular intervals. At full capacity the fishnet can hold upwards of three gallons of water when scooping up fish. While the Brown Pelican is strictly a coastal fisherman, its larger cousin heads inland during the nesting season, primarily to lakes of central Canada and several Rocky Mountain states.

*A*ngel Wings

Wing flapping is a common practice used to shake off feathers wetted during feeding and bathing. The shed water will lighten the load and improve mobility when it is time to fly. With arched back and vigorous treading of the webs, waterfowl like the Wood Duck (*left*) can lift their bodies above the water-line to clear a path for extending the wings, and also provide a fleeting glimpse of the underwing's intricate feathering. Upon swallowing a fish, the Common Loon (*top*)—pictured here in lackluster winter plumage—rinses off from its successful dive. Shorebirds do not swim when bathing but wade up to their waist and dip in the shallows. This bathing beauty is a Short-billed Dowitcher (*above*).

$\mathcal{F}$ast Food

A frenetic lifestyle necessitates a fast-track digestive system to fuel the fire. Birds maintain body temperatures within a normal range of 88° to 104° F, but are careful not to overheat, just as fatal for our feathered friends as for mankind. To sustain such a metabolic rate, birds feed for a great part of each day. Not surprisingly, the excretion of waste matter is a frequent, yet ever so fleeting event. Unlike mammals, birds do not separate solid and liquid waste; the soupy mix exits through one opening, the "cloaca," which also serves in reproductive function. Caught in the act are an Osprey (*left*) and Reddish Egret (*above*). Indigestible matter like bones can be regurgitated, more an issue for a wading bird than a raptor, which can tear off choice parts to eat.

Sleeping Beauty

Catnaps are squeezed in throughout the day to offset taxing activities like flight, foraging, bathing and territory defense. During periods of dozing, the eyes are rarely shut for more than a few seconds at a time, always sneaking a peek of their environs. Individual birds resting in a group like these Roseate Spoonbills (*left*), and a mixed flock of American Avocets and Black-necked Stilts (*below*), do not have to scout as often. The first bird to identify a credible threat will instantly sound the alarm for the benefit of all. When chilled, birds may tuck a leg and the bill into the body to minimize heat loss from unfeathered extremities, as exemplified by these resting pelicans (*following pages*).

CHAPTER FIVE
The Next Generation

And the next time that you raise your gun to needlessly take a feathered life, think of the marvelous little engine that your lead will stifle forever; lower your weapon and look into the clear bright eyes of the bird whose body equals yours in physical perfection, and whose tiny brain can generate a sympathy, a love for its mate, which in sincerity and unselfishness suffers little when compared with human affection.

-Charles
William Beebe

The Penthouse Suite

Towering sea cliffs inaccessible to mammalian predators make ideal nesting sites for seabirds. One such dramatic locale is "Birdrock", a 350-foot Atlantic seastack (*below*) at the tip of Newfoundland's Avalon Peninsula. It hosts the continent's second largest colony of Northern Gannets. Closely related to the tropical boobies who employ similar sky-pointing postures, the gannets make quite a ruckus when nesting in such close quarters (*right*). Less experienced birds will spill over onto small cliff ledges in the vicinity of Black-legged Kittiwakes. Common Murres (*bottom right*) also nest in tight clusters on secluded rock ledges. Interspersed in this mass on the Oregon Coast are a handful of Brandt's Cormorants, black with blue gular patches. There is no murre nest to speak of; a single oblong egg is deposited on bare rock.

*B*est *in Show*

Come spring of the year, it pays handsomely to stand out in a crowd as birds across the continent unabashedly strut their stuff. Surging hormones trigger dramatic transformations, especially in the case of the Snowy Egret (*left*), dressed in a luxuriant coat of nuptial plumes. For the Blue-footed Booby (*below*) a bowed-wing, sky-pointing sidestep does the trick, and when performed with vigor a lady will join in the dance. Courting ducks also use provocative postures to win over a mate. The White-cheeked Pintail (*above*) performs a classic head-up, tail-up display, accompanied by a whistle to his sweetie. Throughout North American marshes the raspy chorus of the Red-winged blackbird (*right*) is a harbinger of spring. Dramatic posturing is all part of the show, as evidenced by the Yellow-headed Blackbird (*following pages*) serenading atop cattails.

Splendor in the Grass

Secluded marshes of bulrush in western lakes spring eternal with the promise of renewal, and a variety of waterbirds, especially the grebes, join in the dance. Reeds are bent over to form a platform on which collected vegetation is added, creating a safe nest beyond the reach of foxes and raccoons. Because the legs of grebes are anchored at the rear of the body (for better underwater propulsion) they are awkward on land and cannot spring into flight like others. Thus a waterside nest allows for a quick escape dive. This Eared Grebe (*right*) standing over its eggs shows the labored stance of a grebe. Hidden in the same marsh are two larger relatives, the Red-necked Grebe (*below*) and Clark's Grebe (*left*). The Clark's is a body double for the more familiar Western Grebe, differing only slightly in bill color and extent of the black cap.

Hide and Seek

Nesting strategies take full advantages of preferred habitat to maximize the chances for successful reproduction. The Common Loon (*left*) typically nests on a secluded lakeshore in thick grasses, but here they are within reach of predators. On occasion a mound of plant debris will be constructed in open water, as this bird has chosen. Off limits to nest raiders, the eggs are still vulnerable to washout from storm waves and motorboat wakes. In equatorial regions, the White-tailed Tropicbird (*right*) lays its single egg in a secure cliff crevice, but it will also nest on the ground when concealed by overhanging vegetation. Far to the north a Western Sandpiper (*below*) broods her tiny camouflaged chicks; note the one resting near her back. Upon hatching from eggs nestled in the tundra, these youngsters are able to walk, zig-zagging through the dense grasses with their mother, feeding and resting at regular intervals. The old-fashioned tree nest (*following pages*) works just fine for many, including the Great Blue Heron (*right*) and Anhinga (*left*). The constant threat posed by prowling snakes, raccoons, and other birds necessitates vigilance.

The Circle of Life

Reproduction is fraught with peril for Black-legged Kittiwakes (*left*) nesting on this remote Alaskan island. A pelagic variety of gull, it builds a small cup nest on tiny ledges of cliffs, small enough to discourage larger predatory gulls from landing to steal the eggs. Any chick that falls out of the nest, or is pushed out by a sibling, is doomed, as in the case of this young kittiwake killed by a Glaucous-winged Gull (*above*). Little is wasted in nature, as nutrients provided by the nestling's body will be recycled to the gull's own chick (*right*), resting near its ground nest. The frenzy of seabird nesting has also drawn the attention of several pairs of Bald Eagles. Curiously, this consummate fisherman will also hunt puffins and kitttiwakes, taken on the wing. This plentiful food source helps to meet the demands of nourishing two chicks (*preceding pages*); kittiwake feathers were found in this nest.

Birthday Suit

Fresh out of the egg, these chicks will grow up fast and fly by summer's end. Like others, the American White Pelican (*above*) hatches out naked. It looks rather reptilian at first glance, which should not be a surprise considering that modern birds share similar features with ancient reptiles. The orange skin will soon sprout white down to help stay warm. These Ring-billed Gulls (*lower right*) do not realize that another mouth will soon join the fray at feeding time. Note the excellent camouflage of this egg, especially important for ground-nesting birds, including the Black Skimmer (*following pages*). Its nest is nothing more than a scrape in the sand. Like these gulls, Canada Geese (*top right*) enter the world with

a warming coat of feathers, albeit damp for a short while. Goslings are highly mobile at the outset, able to swim after mom as she leads them away from danger. Still, menace lurks beneath—snapping turtles and predatory fish.

Light my Fire

The many faces of ritualized courtship ensure that the most virile genes will pass on to the next generation. For wading birds like the Great Blue Heron (*right*) the presentation of a sturdy stick for the nest is a moment of great promise; the attendant bird sky-points with plumes flared in appreciation. Thus the mating sequence is initiated. The bodies of White-tailed Tropicbirds (*below*) almost meld into one during their aerial ballet. The streamer tail feathers will often touch at the height of passion. Drake Hooded Mergansers (*bottom right*) draw circles around a coy hen, strutting, arching and trilling as if their very lives depended on it. Terns score high marks for presentation of a fish, demonstrating a suitor's hunting prowess. Here a male Arctic Tern (*bottom left*) entices a closer view of his catch. Most glorious is the courtship dance of Western Grebes (*following pages*), called "rushing," when a pair or occasional trio shuffles across the lake in tandem.

Follow the Leader

Chicks that become separated from the pack are more likely to be picked off and are thus reluctant to leave their parent's side. With ducks raising a family is solely the job of the hen, her mate having departed upon contributing his genetic code. Duckling mortality is high, which helps to explain why so many eggs are laid. This Mallard (*left*) has lost all but one of her brood in the span of a few days; most likely snapping turtles grabbed its siblings. Swans seem to be more successful in raising large families. Mute Swans (*above*) care for their signets as a team, the highly aggressive male serving as an effective guard as mom totes them around. Any intruder will have to face a bold charge on the wing. The Pacific Loon (*below*) rears just one or two chicks during a nesting season. Baby loons rely on a parent delivering meals of fresh fish and aquatic insects, very labor-intensive work compared to a self-feeding duckling or signet.

The Comeback Kid

The glorious profile of a winged Osprey (*left*), here transporting nesting material, is a familiar sight on six continents, earning it the distinction of the world's most widely distributed raptor. Its North American status was precarious just a short time ago, but since the banning of the agricultural pesticide DDT in 1972 the Osprey has proven its resilience. Now it is a common resident of our coastlines, estuaries, lakes, and rivers. Like other large, fish-eating birds, Ospreys accumulated toxic concentrations of this and other chemicals by repeated consumption of fish contaminated by agricultural runoff. The net result was compromised calcium intake, translating into weak eggshells that cracked under the weight of an incubating parent. A key component of the fish hawk's recovery has been the installation of nesting platforms (*right*) in depleted areas. Fond of man-made structures, they also nest on duck blinds, channel markers, utility poles and chimneys, though trees work well enough. An average of two young are fledged after two months of prodigious fish consumption (*above*), with two or three meals daily.

Joy Ride

Grebes are celebrated for the endearing practice of transporting young backside, nestled between the wings—as do loons, swans, coots, and a few others. These species are the Eared Grebe (*left*) and Red-necked Grebe (*above*). Such parental care helps to keep the chicks warm, conserve energy, and reduce access by predatory fish, turtles, and gulls. In a moment of crisis, the buoyant chicks clamp down on their parents' feathers and hang on for a wet ride along the underwater escape route. As the chicks gain confidence they will spend more time paddling around with the adults, who must make many dives daily to keep the family well fed. Once back at the nest there is no better place to sleep than on mom's soft back.

The Young and the Restless

Unlike tree-nesting species like the Great Egret (*right*), the young of ground-nesters are highly mobile within days (if not hours) of hatching. Pictured here (*clockwise from far right*) are a Mew Gull, Sandhill Cranes, Killdeer, American Coots, and Lesser Scaup. Greater Flamingo chicks (*preceding pages*) flock together in a nursery group, usually flanked by a few adult guardians.

Coast To Coast

We stand now where two roads diverge. But unlike the roads in Robert Frost's familiar poem, they are not equally fair. The road we have long been traveling is deceptively easy, a smooth super highway on which we progress with great speed, but at its end lies disaster. The other fork of the road—the one "less traveled by"—offers our last, our only chance to reach a destination that assures the preservation of our earth.

—Rachel Carson

Some Like it Hot

Nothing cures a case of the winter blues quite like a trip to the Sunshine State, as evidenced by the annual pilgrimage of birders and their feathered quarry. Florida's climate, hydrology, and peninsular shape combine to create birdwatching paradise. With so much public land set aside for wildlife, this vast state offers a bounty of waterbird hotspots up and down the Gulf and Atlantic Coasts. The sub-tropical climate harbors a profusion of plant life (in excess of 1,000 varieties of seed-bearing plants) that in turn shelter and feed a vast web of life. Each fall a huge volume of North American waterfowl, shorebirds, waders and seabirds migrate to Florida for an extended visit. Pictured here are a Common Moorhen (*above*) navigating a maze of mangrove roots, a pair of Great Blue Heron chicks (*below*) cradled in a pepper tree nest, and a Sora (*left*) foraging under a canopy of lush emergent vegetation. Huge concentrations of wading birds (*following pages*) may be observed feasting when fish get trapped in the shallows of shrinking ponds.

Northern Exposure

One can only imagine the wonder of weary pioneers a century ago, having reached Alaska and discovering a chilled Eden featuring waterbirds by the millions. Harvesting gold proved to be a daunting challenge, but not the incalculable volume of biomass—fish, crustaceans, mollusks, insects and grubs—mined by the birds for eons. Fortunately most of Alaska's vast areas of wilderness are still unspoiled, hosting tremendous numbers of waterfowl, shorebirds and seabirds. Many travel thousands of miles to nest here each summer. Diverse habitats include icy lakes where a King Eider (*right*) might linger, lush coastal gardens of fireweed, patrolled by a Glaucous-winged Gull (*above*), and the endless expanse of featureless tundra, home to a strutting Pectoral Sandpiper (*below*) on the North Slope.

Cape May Getaway

Any season is a good time for birds and birdwatchers to rendezvous for a little romance in the delightful seaside town of Cape May. Here the Delaware Bay and Atlantic Ocean meet as New Jersey's southern peninsula tapers to a point, a well-known migration bottleneck. The Sanderling (*left*) is a familiar sight from fall to spring. Patient examination of a freshwater marsh may yield a treasure like the King Rail (*below*), who will not pose for long out in the open. Several species of waterbirds breed on the Jersey shore, including the Black Skimmer (*lower left*). The real showstoppers are the migratory shorebirds (*following pages*). Northbound spring migrants, including the Red Knot and Ruddy Turnstone, visit the Cape each May to fuel up on horseshoe crab eggs for their long trek to Arctic breeding grounds.

The Lake District

Northern wilderness lakes, gouged out by retreating glaciers some 10,000 years ago, harbor abundant food resources tailor-made for waterbirds. None is more beloved than the Common Loon (*below*), whose chilling calls embody the very essence of the wild. Loons nest on large, quiet lakes from New England north and west into Alaska. Over the course of the summer, several thousand fish may be caught to adequately nourish a family of four. The goliath Trumpeter Swan (*right*) once ranged across the northern continent as well, but reckless hunting brought it to the brink of extinction a century ago. Thanks to strong conservation efforts, they now number some 15,000 birds, the majority residing in Alaska. This family of vegetarians was raised on a Minnesota lake, one of several areas where Trumpeters have been reintroduced.

𝒢ulf Breeze

Mention the Lone Star State to any serious birder, and their eyes light up with anticipation. Upwards of 600 bird species can be seen throughout Texas, more than any other state. Waterbirds are diverse and plentiful, saturating a long perimeter of beaches, bays, marshes, ponds, and rivers. Few sightings generate more excitement than that of a Whooping Crane (*right*), here hunting for blue crabs in the company of Roseate Spoonbills. Aransas National Wildlife Refuge's sprawling salt marshes are the primary winter home of these endangered cranes, numbering less than 200 wild birds. Freshwater wetlands also teem with life; here the recalcitrant American Bittern (*top right*) surveys a ditch where crayfish move cautiously. Strolling the beach may turn up a shorebird like the Snowy Plover (*left*) or a flock of Laughing Gulls and Royal Terns (*above*). Can you find the Sandwich Tern with a yellow-tipped bill?

California Dreamin'

W here land meets sea on California's magnificent coastline, nature frames an inspiring picture at every turn, as with this Coronado Beach sunset (*right*). Estuaries like San Diego's Mission Bay are routinely stalked by waders like the Black-crowned Night-Heron (*above*) and shorebirds like the Whimbrel. (*below*). The blue Pacific makes a lovely backdrop for Western Brown Pelicans, Double-crested and Brandt's Cormorants (*preceding pages*). Marine mammals also thrive on the California coast. Sea lion's bask on Monterey's "Bird Rock" (*upper left*) as a pair of Heermann's Gulls pass while elephant seals in San Simeon face-off with hungry Western Gulls (*lower right*) feasting on afterbirth.

$\mathcal{T}$he North Atlantic Fleet

$\mathcal{B}$eneath the frigid North Atlantic surf a splendid drama unfolds... days of longer sunlight trigger an explosion of phytoplankton (minute drifting plants), grazed upon by the zooplankton (floating animals like fish and shellfish larvae). In turn larger creatures are sustained, including the schooling fish, up the food chain. The seabirds are clued in, of course. At strategic locations along the coast prolific colonies of fishing birds stage each summer to reap the bounty and raise the next generation. Cape St. Mary's (*left*) in Newfoundland is one such wondrous spectacle, where the cliffs become veritable fish factories as Northern Gannets, Black-legged Kittiwakes, and Common Murres process the day's catch. Off Maine's northern coast, Machias Seal Island (*this page*) is blanketed by a half-dozen varieties of seabird, including the Razorbill (*above*), a stocky auk with a penguin-like posture, and the Atlantic Puffin (*below*), delivering protein to the nest.

South of the Border

Sheltered in the verdant habitats of coastal Mexico, one finds an interesting mix of wintering species from the north and year-round tropical residents. Two reclusive herons that do not venture north of the border are the Boat-billed Heron (*below left*) and the Bare-throated Tiger Heron (*below right*). The shadow world of mangrove swamps suits their needs well with ample fish and dense cover for hunting and roosting. A "jungle boat" trip along the San Cristobal River near San Blas may also turn up a Least Grebe (*above*), the smallest of North America's seven grebe species. This freshwater fisherman can also be seen in South Texas, the northern extent of its range. Secluded Pacific islands like Isabela host spectacular seabird colonies. The boobies, tropicbirds, and others that occasionally venture to the U.S. coast (delighting birders to no end) start their lives in tropical Edens like Isabela. Here an incubating Magnificent Frigatebird (*right*) shares a tree with the flamboyant green iguana. The giant lizard has no immediate interest in her eggs, but favors a high perch so nearby females can gaze at his magnificent profile, especially the sexy wattle under his chin that he likes to shake for all to see.

ℒand of Pleasant Living

The fabled Chesapeake Bay is North America's largest estuary, with an astonishing 12,000 miles of tidal shoreline. When Captain John Smith first explored the Bay in 1608 on behalf of the King of England, he was enraptured with the pristine ecosystem, later commenting: "heaven and earth never agreed better to frame a place better for man's habitation...." Undoubtedly he was impressed by the abundant bird life that harvested the Bay's seemingly endless resources. Legend has it that abundant fish could be scooped up with a frying pan. Waterfowl like the Tundra Swan (*right*) are drawn to the Chesapeake each fall, taking this exit on the Atlantic Flyway for winter's duration. Among the region's breeding waterbirds is the Wood Duck (*above*), favoring secluded backwaters with plenty of cover vegetation. Many bird populations are greatly reduced from historic levels due to overharvesting, habitat loss and degradation of water quality. The substantial loss of submerged aquatic vegetation is of particular concern, as it feeds waterfowl and shelters young fish, crabs, and a host of others. A multi-state campaign to restore the Bay proceeds at a snail's pace as the watershed's population continues to soar, a prophecy fulfilled.

Cliffhanger

A colorful cast of characters stand sentry on St. Paul Island's craggy cliffs, overlooking fertile fishing grounds. Castaways from mainland Alaska, the Pribilof Islands are but mere dots on the Bering Sea radar, but for seabirds of the North Pacific these granite outcrops are bright beacons, hosting the Northern Hemisphere's largest bird colony, two million strong. The towering cliffs are riddled with nooks, crevices, and ledges where eggs can be securely deposited, and therein lies the islands' appeal. Among the dozen species of seabird found here during summer months are (*clockwise from right*) Northern Fulmar, Parakeet Auklet, Thick-billed Murre, Least Auklet, Red-faced Cormorant, Horned Puffin and (*preceding pages*) Crested Auklet (*left*) and Tufted Puffin (*right*). Visitors are welcome at the two inhabited islands, which also feature beautiful wildflowers, nesting songbirds, arctic fox, and a fur seal colony.

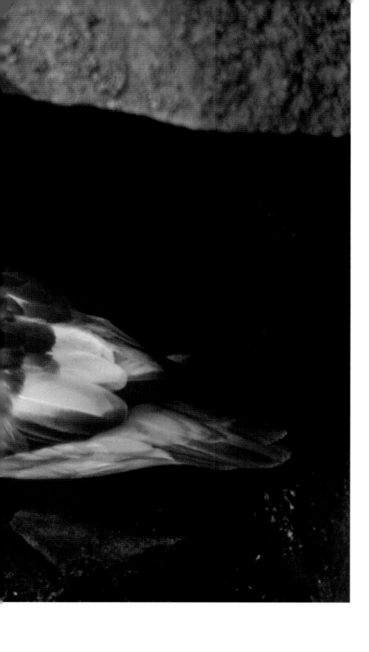

Churchill
Congregation

Canada's storied outpost on the Hudson Bay, Churchill was once a major fur-trading station. It now lures crowds of naturalists in search of autumn's polar bears and summer's breeding birds. Vast stretches of sub-arctic tundra make ideal habitat for concealing precious eggs laid on the ground, while summer's copious insect and aquatic life provide ample food stores to nourish another generation. Considering the extreme weath-

er that goes with the territory, Churchill's bird list is rather robust. Among the waterbirds to be seen are (*counterclockwise from right*) the Parasitic Jaeger, Common Eider, Stilt Sandpiper, Red-necked Phalarope and Hudsonian Godwit. Because of an excellent road system, it is possible to explore the Hudson Bay's rocky shoreline, tundra, lakes, ponds, marshes, and even boreal forest, all within several miles of town. Few places can compete with Churchill's diversity and convenience. Nonetheless, the enthusiasm of all those birders and photographers will be tempered by the fickle weather (often cold, wet, and dreary) and the tundra's scourge—relentless mosquitoes and blackflies.

Snow Geese (*below*) and Sandhill Cranes (*right*), min-
d, framed by the lovely Magdalena Mountains—the
of North America's seasoned birders. Ironically, one
waterbird destinations lies within the New Mexico
National Wildlife Refuge borders a 12-mile strip of
miles south of Albuquerque. Manmade impoundments
de a winter haven for upwards of 12,000 Sandhill
se, 20,000 ducks and flocks of blackbirds (*bottom*
bitat sustains a good variety of bird life throughout
winter assemblage of migrants that steal the show.
ry roosts and harvested fields in raucous flight (*pre-*
delight of birders, photographers and predators.

On Assignment...

Photo by Arthur Morris

Cape May, New Jersey

Photo by self

Middleton Island, Alaska

Photo by Jessica Earle

La Jolla, California

Photo by Bob Rinker

Estero Lagoon, Florida

Photo by Kristie Evans

Patterson Park, Maryland

37 major trips, four countries, five years, 185 species photographed, 200,000 slides, many sore backs, mucho dinero... and memories to last a life time.

Isabel Island, Mexico

Photo by Jessica Earle

Hudson Bay, Canada

Photo by Moose Petterson

Isabel Island, Mexico

Photo by Jessica Earle

Druid Hill Park, Maryland

Photo by Kristie Evans

Lake Alamoosook, Maine

Photo by Innkeeper

On Assignment...

Bob Rinker at the Venice Rookery

Armando Santiago at Isabel Island, Mexico

Jessica Earle at Bosque del Apache

Jean Keene and Kristie Evans, Homer

Arthur Morris and a student, Cape May

Gerda Deterer with an orphan

A world of thanks to those individuals who provided so much
encouragment and assistance throughout the project... this is your book too.

Jessica Earle with dinner, Mexico

Kristie Evans with elephant seals, California

Ralph Paonessa and Chris Gamel, Nome

Bob Rinker finds a snake, Estero Lagoon

Rhonda Kidd and myself, Newfoundland

Verena Gill (blue) and researchers, Alaska

Photography Notes

Cover Black Skimmer
Merritt Island NWR, Florida
(April 1998)
*Nikon F5, 600 mm f4 lens
with 1.4x TC, Fuji Provia 100*

Upon noticing feeding skimmers looping the shallows of a pond along the wildlife drive, I stationed myself on the bank. What a great opportunity to put my brand new 600 mm autofocus lens to the test. I was able to fire off several series of birds slicing across the still waters right in front of me in soft morning light. With 840 mm of effective magnification (through the addition of a 1.4x teleconverter), it was a challenge to keep the bird centered while panning on a monopod. Nonetheless, the results were compelling; Nikon's dynamic autofocus technology was terrific, locking onto a target accelerating across the frame. I try to avoid cutting off wingtips in flight, but here it doesn't bother me as the bird's open red bill is the focal point.

Page 1 Reddish Egret
Estero Lagoon, Florida
(December 2000)
*Nikon F5, 600 mm f4 lens,
Kodak E100 VS*

Feeding Reddish Egrets are very entertaining to watch, but a challenge to photograph successfully. Their sudden jerky movements—wings flapping and bodies twisting—present a problem for shooters like me who prefer a tight crop on their subjects. Autofocus can also be confused as the bird sidesteps the targeted focus sensors. The sun had just gone down and there was little color in the sky. Fortunately, at Estero the high-rise condominiums reflect soft pastels in the lagoon's shallow waters. I positioned myself such that the egret crossed into a sweet band of orange, simulating a beautiful sunset over the beach.

Page 2 Great Blue Heron
Wakulla Springs,
Florida (January 2000)
*Nikon F5, 600 mm f4
lens, Fuji Velvia 50*

This shot was a bonus toward the end of a somewhat disappointing jungle boat ride at Wakulla Springs on Florida's panhandle. The scenery was rich, but the skies were a somber grey and it was bitter cold. We found some Hooded Mergansers, the targeted species for the mission, but they were skittish like most wild ducks approached by a boat. Heading back to the dock, I noticed a statuesque heron anchored to the base of an ancient bald cypress draped with Spanish moss. I had hoped for such a habitat portrait of a Great Blue Heron at the outset of the project in 1998 and it took me by complete surprise on this frosty morning.

Page 4 Bald Eagle
Homer, Alaska (March 2003) *Nikon F5, 80-400 f4.5 zoom lens, Kodak E100 VS*

This is one of my all-time favorite shots. Several hundred Bald Eagles congregate on the Homer Spit each winter due to a windfall of fish scraps provided by a local who feeds the birds daily in the winter. After the morning frenzy, I strolled the beach near the Eagle Lady's home as birds tend to hang out there for much of the day. I initially did tight shots of this beautiful immature bird perched on driftwood, but I saw the potential for a great habitat portrait with the mountains in the background. I laid down on the beach to sandwich the bird against the snow-capped mountains. I shot in the 300 mm range on my vibration-reduction zoom and chose a small aperture (probably f11) for increased depth of field.

Page 6 Wood Ducks
Patterson Park,
Maryland (April 2001)
*Nikon F5, 600 mm f4
lens, Kodak E100 VS*

Throughout the Rhapsody project, I shot copious amounts of film on Wood Ducks in Patterson Park, located just two miles from my home in downtown Baltimore. Four or five pairs breed at the small lake in the park, and since these woodies take handouts from the locals, they are more approachable than typical wild ducks. The year before, I saw ducks perched high up in trees with nesting cavities, but didn't get any shots. In the spring of 2001, I made a point of walking the park with the hopes of seeing a pair perched on a limb. This tree had a big cavity and got lots of attention from several pairs. I was delighted to have one drake perch when a second flew in for a look.

Page 8 Roseate Spoonbills
Ding Darling NWR,
Florida (February 1993)
*Nikon F3, 600 mm f4
lens, Fuji Provia 100*

About five years prior to this project, I took a trip to Sanibel Island for a romantic getaway with my girlfriend. I remember traveling to Ding Darling with my folks as a kid and delighting in all the birds. Now that I was behind the wheel, there would be many trips to the refuge that week in 1993. On one memorable shoot, a flock of spoonbills settled in at dusk along the cross-dike. The light was dim, necessitating shutter speeds of 1/8 second and slower. I knew that the preening birds would blur, creating an impressionistic feel. Earlier that day, I met a confident, bearded photographer by the name of Arthur Morris autographing his first book. Little did I know that we would become friends years later.

Page 10 Brown Boobies
Isabel Island, Mexico
(December 2000) *Nikon
F100, 28-200 f4.5 lens,
Kodak E100 VS*

I hired a local fisherman and bird enthusiast from the seaside town of San Blas to take me to Isabel to photograph nesting tropical seabirds. Fortunately, I was able to secure a permit from the Mexican wildlife authorities to photograph on this uninhabited island. The Brown Boobies nested close to our camp and I visited them several times a day. This remote Pacific Island gets very few human visitors, but the birds were surprisingly trusting. I sat on the ground for an eye-level habitat shot when this male leaned toward me, nearly touching the lens with his bill. I focused my wide angle on mom with her chick and went for maximum depth of field with an aperture of f16. I tried my best to keep a little sky in the composition.

Page 12 Sandhill Cranes & Snow Geese
Bosque del Apache NWR, New Mexico (November 2000) *Nikon F5, 600 mm f4 lens with 1.4x TC, Fuji Provia 100*

I was concentrating on incoming groups of cranes descending onto a freshly harvested cornfield to join in the feeding frenzy. Suddenly the field exploded into raucous flight right next to the road where a battalion of photographers lined up like a firing squad. More than likely, a marauding coyote spooked the group. I do not remember consciously framing this scene... my instincts took over as I hunted for a shot in the melee. Cranes and geese do not fly together under normal circumstances, so this was a golden opportunity. I like to think that the featured crane is calling out to its mate separated in the shuffle, but such speculation is a wild guess.

Page 14 Dunlin
Stone Harbor Point,
New Jersey (May 2000)
*Nikon N90s, 600 mm
f4 lens with 2x TC,
Fuji Velvia 50*

Halfway through the project, I really became enamored with shorebirds, although I knew what back-breaking work it was to make interesting close-ups. Even with a huge lens, one still has to be absurdly close to make a decent portrait. The Dunlin in breeding plumage intrigued me and I wanted one for the book. This bird was feeding along the backside of Stone Harbor's expansive point. The odds of getting a nice portrait of a single bird are greater than one in a group. For the longest time, this bird would not let me get close, despite a cautious approach. Finally, it stopped to preen and rest as I inched my way in on sore, sandy knees. With the help of a 2x teleconverter, I was finally in range.

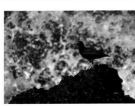

Page 15 Black Oystercatcher
Point Lobos, California
(January 1999) *Nikon
F5, 600 mm f4 lens,
Fuji Sensia 100*

The Black Oystercatcher was at the top of my list on my first trip to the West Coast in 1999. Just south of Carmel is Point Lobos State Park, where one can watch waves crashing onto boulders. I was inspired to explore the beach, examining tidal pools and their host of colorful inhabitants, especially the anemones. I didn't have to wait long to hear the shrill call of the Black Oystercatcher... a pair was scampering over wet boulders. The rocks were essentially black, so the shots didn't excite me too much. One of the birds disappeared behind a large rock and I followed. He eventually settled on a high perch with a blue background. Every so often a big wave would shoot up a wall of whitewater.

Page 16 Black-bellied Plover
Nome, Alaska (June
2001) *Nikon F5, 600
mm f4 lens with 2x
TC, Fuji Velvia 50*

When I first viewed this slide, it did not do much for me, as it was made on a gloomy day in poor light. I used fill flash, but it did not kick in enough light at such a great distance with 1200 mm. We scanned the image at home and voila, it popped on the screen nice and bright. It wanted to be published. This handsome male plover and its mate were scurrying across the tundra amidst their nesting territory when our group of five eventually pinpointed the nest. We carefully approached the nest, keeping low to the ground, waiting for the bird to return to incubate. I noticed the delicate yellow tundra wildflowers and hoped the bird would strike a pose there as he moved closer to the nest.

Page 16 Glaucous-winged Gull
Homer, Alaska
(January 1999) *Nikon
F5, 600 mm f4 lens,
Fuji RMS (400)*

I didn't expect to see such a large gathering of gulls on my first trip to Homer as it was the depth of winter and downright miserable. There was little to go around after the eagles had their share of the handouts at the Eagle Lady's home. Late one afternoon, I strolled the rocky beach at the tip of Homer Spit, hoping to see an otter. Some large gulls were hanging around so I returned to the restaurant for some extra bread. Just like gulls from my neck of the woods, they were interested in the offerings. This gull was landing in the surf to claim a handout. I call him the one-armed bandit as his left wing is practically invisible as it points directly at the lens. I had no idea that it would turn out this way.

Rhapsody In Blue

Page 16 American Bittern
Brazos Bend Park, Texas (March 2000) *Nikon F5, 600 mm f4 lens with 1.4x TC, Fuji Provia 100*

On our whirlwind Texas safari, we made a side trip to Brazos Bend State Park, a little out of the way from our coastal tour, but very enticing based on a write-up in a guide book. The vegetation was lush, but birds along the river were distant and few. A side trail that paralleled a flooded ditch looked promising. We encountered some birders and stopped for a chat. An American Bittern was lurking perhaps 200 yards yonder and we thanked our compatriots for the tip. After a heart-pounding search, we found the prize just 25 feet from the trail hunkered down in a thicket. After an hour of nice poses in the lush greenery, he started to feed on crayfish.

Page 17 Green-winged & Cinnamon Teal
Newport Back Bay, California (January 2003) *Nikon F5, 600 mm f4 lens with 2x TC, Kodak E100 VS*

There is a tiny pool by the road that connects via a narrow passage to the main channel at the Newport Back Bay Ecological Preserve. Maybe twenty feet across, this spot has provided countless hours of exceptional duck photography on two different trips. I had heard about this place in 1999 while on Artie's workshop in Southern California, but the reserve was closed off due to road problems. Two years later, we returned and Artie introduced the group to this little magic pond where I photographed my very first Cinnamon Teal. Two years hence, I returned and the ducks were still plentiful. They come here after feeding in the refuge to preen, bathe, and rest.

Page 17 American White Pelican
Lake Manitoba, Canada (June 1998) *Nikon F5, 600 mm f4 lens, Fuji Sensia 100*

This shot was made from a pop-up blind set up for me by my guide, Harry Harris, who hired a local fisherman to take us out to a remote island rookery of pelicans and cormorants. As soon as my assistants returned to the boat anchoring a good bit offshore, the pelicans returned to their nests, some just a few feet away. Most of the birds were too close to shoot with the big lens, but this one nest looked promising. I only got a clean look at it when a neighboring bird repositioned her bill and thus gave me an unobstructed view. When the tiny chick popped out from under its huge parent, I knew that I had my moment. What a blessing and a privilege to spend several hours in this avian Eden.

Page 17 Tundra Swans
Magothy River, Maryland (February 2001) *Nikon F5, 600 mm f4 lens, Fuji Velvia 50*

A friend tipped me off on a local couple who fed swans all winter long on the Chesapeake Bay about a half-hour's drive from my house. I was elated to receive an invitation to view their waterfowl. For several winters, I returned numerous times to document the colorful assemblage of swans, geese and ducks. The Tundra Swans and most of the duck species would stay far out in the river until corn was thrown out for the daily feeding. With group shots like this, I try to avoid cutting off part of a bird from the frame's edge, so I carefully watched how the swans were dispersing through the viewfinder to find the right moment. Fortunately, they lined up with the rising sun for a glorious Chesapeake sunrise.

Page 18 Canada Goose
Magothy River, Maryland (January 2001) *Nikon F5, 600 mm f4 Lens with 1.4x TC, Kodak E100 VS*

On this afternoon, I was throwing out corn for the ducks and swans at Bryan's pier on the Chesapeake Bay. Some days they were reluctant to come in, depending on the wind and other variables, but a few dozen geese were always close by. Although I have plenty of goose shots, the light was so pretty that I couldn't resist a few more. When the geese raise their heads out of the water upon dunking for corn, water would drip off the bill and that's the shot that I was going for. At one point, a golden gander raised his massive wings to flap and I quickly panned the camera to attempt a shot. I didn't have time to take off the teleconverter, but this tight framing still seems to work for some reason.

Page 19 Great Egret
St. Augustine, Florida (March 1998) *Nikon F5, 600 mm f4 lens, Fuji Sensia 100*

The St. Augustine Alligator Farm offers a bounty of photo opportunities during the nesting season when various species of wading birds converge around the large pond's perimeter of trees. Several Great Egrets were displaying that March morning and I needed to pick one to concentrate on. From my initial position, all of the birds had a background of distracting branches. I saw a sliver of blue sky through the canopy and repositioned to make that my background for this Don Juan advertising for a partner. The display involves a lot of neck contortions; I tried to click at the peak arching. I was also drawn to this bird's beautiful ruby eye, a condition that may only last for a week or two during the height of breeding.

Page 20 Brown Pelican
La Jolla, California (January 2003) *Nikon F5, 600 mm f4 lens with 1.4x TC, Kodak E100 VS*

This was one of those 15-roll mornings at La Jolla when a large group of stunning Western Brown Pelicans lounge at the cliffs bathed in gorgeous light. There are so many potential shots to go for that you really have to concentrate on one at a time to avoid getting flustered. This bird was on a ledge by himself preening his shaggy coat to the delight of a half-dozen photographers. This pose, communing with God as it would appear, looks rather static, but the bird's head was in constant motion. This exact positioning of the head lasted perhaps one second, if that. When shooting action sequences, it's best to lock your eye on the subject and keep your finger on the trigger.

Page 22 Trumpeter Swan
Hennepin Parks, Minnesota (September 1999) *Nikon F5, 600 mm f4 Lens with 1.4x TC, Fuji Provia 100*

It took a number of phone calls to track down a good area to photograph wild Trumpeter Swans. A woman with Hennepin Parks near Minneapolis was very receptive to my call and I scheduled a trip to this sanctuary where the birds have been reintroduced. She guided me to a secluded lake graced by a family of six swans. Over the course of several hours, the birds became acclimated and I was able to move around at will without disturbing them. This adult was swimming close to shore. Since I already had full-body portraits, I challenged myself for a different look, dropping down low where the lakeside grasses framed his head. Notice how the eye is visible through the blades.

Page 22 Black-necked Stilt
Lake Kissimmee, Florida (April 1999) *Nikon F5, 600 mm f4 Lens with 1.4x TC, Kodak E100 VS*

I hired an airboat tour operator for two days to ferry me around this secluded lake in central Florida with the hope of getting close to Snail Kites. The lake was so expansive and remote that the birds have little exposure to people, and it seemed that they should be shy. As it turned out, we got close-up views of over a dozen species, surprising considering the boat's noisy motor. We hung out with this stilt for nearly an hour as it fed in the shallows. I saw the clump of green stalks and waited for the bird to wade through for a compelling habitat shot. Stilts are a bird that is best photographed when the sun is low; otherwise the red eye photographs very dark, if not black.

Page 23 Horned Grebe
Churchill, Canada (June 1998) *Nikon F5, 600 mm f4 Lens with 1.4x TC, Fuji Sensia 100*

I purchased my first pair of chest waders for this Churchill trip at the project's outset. Little did I know that we would actually be putting them to the test. A pair of Horned Grebes were nesting somewhere on this small frigid pond. Our group of five waded out to waist level before getting close enough to the bank that the birds favored. We choreographed our movements based on their body language, stopping our approach whenever the birds seemed alarmed. I'm amazed that we were able to get close at all considering how intimidating it was for five giants to invade their private pond. An hour went by before a grebe gave me a wonderful habitat portrait, his red eye lighting up the scene.

Page 23 Black-crowned Night-Heron
Bolsa Chica Reserve, California (January 1999) *Nikon N90s, 600 mm f4 Lens with 1.4x TC, Kodak E100 SW*

Walking along a path at Bolsa Chica, I caught a glimpse of this resting heron on my periphery. Since the bird seemed to be hiding in the grasses, certainly not seeking any attention, I put him in the lower corner to render him as he appeared, a shy marsh stalker. In many places, such a bird would have taken off the moment I stopped to have a look. However, Bolsa Chica gets so many visitors on the designated pathways that the birds accept people as part of the scene. After I slowed down enough to connect with this bird, I found another in a short tree not twenty yards away, which I surely would have missed at my brisk pace had I not switched to Night-Heron speed.

Page 24 Surf Scoter
Bolsa Chica Reserve, California (January 2003) *Nikon F5, 600 mm f4 Lens with 1.4x TC, Fuji Provia 100*

Bolsa Chica is a wonderful refuge to make photographs of the Surf Scoter, a shy and usually distant sea duck. On each of my three trips to California, I was able to get close to this handsome species at Bolsa Chica. Working my way around the lagoon, I noticed a group of a half-dozen scoters acting particularly frisky. I remember looking through the viewfinder at one drake and inviting him to "bring it on." Call it good intuition, but moments later he flew right toward me from about 100 yards away and touched down for a dramatic splash landing maybe 60 feet away. It is certainly not everyday when shoots play out in such a pleasing manner... what an amazing God!

Photography Notes

Page25 Atlantic Puffin
Machias Seal Island, Maine
(July 2001) *Nikon F5, 80-400 mm f4.5 lens, Kodak E100 VS*

This image was taken from one of the photo blinds set up on the island amidst the puffin colony. Machias Seal Island is the only place in the U. S. where visitors can set foot on a puffin island and photograph at close-range. Wildlife biologists escort visitors during the summer nesting season to the blinds for a 45-minute shift. Once photographers close the door, the seabirds return to their roosts within feet of the shacks. It is delightful to hear the pitter-patter of puffin feet on the roof just two feet above. When shooting portraits of birds, I will frequently keep my eye and finger at the ready for fleeting moments such as this yawn. When I got the slide back, I was pleasantly surprised by the bird's spongy orange mouth parts, a very subtle detail when viewed from a distance.

Page26 Whooping Crane
Lake Kissimmee, Florida
(April 1999) *Nikon F5, 600 mm f4 with 1.4x TC, Fuji RMS (200)*

I am a strong believer in signs, such as the Middleton Fish Camp on Lake Kissimmee being a good area to view Whooping Cranes, a tip I heard on the grapevine. After a successful shoot with the Snail Kites, I asked Captain Ben to make the long run to Middleton Fish Camp. Lake Kissimmee is a vast wetland and the chances of finding free-ranging Whooping Cranes are a long-shot at best. None were seen where I had hoped, but on the return trip, four white specks on the horizon piqued my interest. A closer look yielded two pair of the statuesque crane feeding on the lakeshore. I got off the boat a good distance away and worked my way toward the birds. One of the pairs suddenly took flight and I took aim.

Page27 American Dipper
Lower Santiam River, Oregon
(May 2001) *Nikon F5, 600 mm f4 lens with 1.4x TC,. Kodak E100 VS*

I was determined to get an American Dipper for this book—a strange songbird that dives into whitewater streams and gathers aquatic food. I asked around and was referred to the Lower Santiam River as prime habitat for the American Dipper and Harlequin Duck. I searched the river at every pullover, but was at a loss to see any birds. Hours later, I came upon a small bridge to a neighborhood and decided to have a look. This time, my gut feeling proved correct as a few drab little birds perched on soaked boulders. A fledgling dipper was being fed by its parent. To get the proper vantage point, I scaled down a nearly vertical six-foot rock face with my equipment in hand.

Page29 American Avocet
Freezeout Lake, Montana (June 1999) *Nikon F5, 600 mm f4 lens with 1.4x TC, Kodak E100 VS*

This American Avocet is performing a nest distraction display to lure me away from its eggs by feigning a broken wing. Fortunately, I saw where the bird was sitting so I knew where not to walk and risk stepping on the well-camouflaged eggs. The alkaline flats and grasslands surrounding Freezeout Lake host many shorebirds... something I didn't realize when booking the trip to photograph grebes. When working nesting shorebirds and birds in general, it is very important to pay attention to the temperature. If it is too hot or too cold, the untended eggs could be compromised. If my presence keeps a bird off the nest, I need to limit this shoot to just a few minutes under harsh conditions.

Page25 Long-billed Curlew
Bolsa Chica, California
(January 1999) *Nikon F5, 600 mm f4 with 1.4x TC, Fuji Velvia 50*

Opportunities for flight shots of the Long-billed Curlew are rare, no matter how much time you spend in the field. At Bolsa Chica Ecological Reserve, I noticed that the curlew and others fly over the dike at the floodgates. I set up at the dike on two afternoons, the sun over my shoulder. A few shorebirds passed, but I wasn't able to get the autofocus to lock onto them. Shorebirds are very fast flyers and relatively small in the frame. With just an hour of pretty light left, I gave up on the shot and moved down the trail where some Northern Pintails were feeding. From out of nowhere, a Long-billed Curlew made a dramatic landing on the near shore, bathed in beautiful light.

Page27 Magnificent Frigatebird
Isabel Island, Mexico (December 2000) *Nikon F100, 80-400 mm f4.5 lens, Kodak E100 VS*

Once you've made the considerable effort of getting yourself onto a remote Pacific Island covered with nesting seabirds, shots like this are easy. Like other seabirds on this island, the frigatebirds are very trusting of humans, making close-ups a sure thing. It is still important, however, to watch the birds' body language and approach with respect. This male is advertising for some female companionship in a short tree near the beach. As with almost all other shots in the book, I trusted Nikon's 3D matrix metering to determine the proper exposure and shot with zero compensation. This shot was handheld in the 400 mm range of my brand new vibration reduction zoom lens.

Page28 Osprey
Tred Avon River, Maryland (July 2002) *Nikon F5, 600 mm f4 lens with 2x TC, Kodak E100 VS*

The Osprey is one of my all-time favorite birds. Indeed, my first wild bird inspirations as a kid were Osprey on the Chesapeake Bay and on vacations to Florida. Having a pair take up residence at my parents' home on Maryland's Eastern Shore was a dream come true. I shot this pair over three nesting seasons. After trying to nest on a chimney, they finally settled on a nesting platform installed fifty feet from the bank. I love how these fledglings, gorgeous with big orange eyes and flecked plumage, flank their mother. This nest is one of my favorites to shoot because I can frame in trees across the creek as a soft green background. I can also lower myself on the bank for a blue sky background for flight shots.

Page29 Least Terns
Stone Harbor, New Jersey (May 2000) *Nikon N90s, 600 mm f4 lens with 2x TC, Fuji Provia 100*

A talented photographer from Cape May by the name of Kevin Karlson was kind enough to show me a nesting area for Least Terns. I met him two years prior at the Cape May Meadows while photographing a King Rail. Several species of waterbird nest on the sand at Stone Harbor, including a handfull of endangered Least Terns. Once a territory was identified, I waited for the birds to return. During courtship, the male presents a series of fish to demonstrate his fishing skills. Later on I noticed a nearly invisible egg just a few feet away from this spot. The colonies are roped off to prevent accidental trampling by beachcombers and their dogs, but this pair was off by itself in an open area of beach.

Page26 Mottled Ducks
Lake Kissimmee, Florida (April 1999) *Nikon F5, 600 mm f4 with 1.4x TC, Kodak E100 VS*

This was a bonus shot while looking for Snail Kites aboard our airboat with the noisy motor. Although this lake offered a high concentration of nesting Snail Kites, all sorts of waterbirds made their home here. When I first saw this hen in the water, I was not too excited as it appeared to be a Mallard. The captain informed me that this was a Mottled Duck. Anytime a new species shows up, my interest soars. When she exited the water, I was delighted to see several ducklings in tow and managed to fire off two or three frames before they disappeared into the vegetation. With flat bottoms, airboats are very stable platforms to shoot from, even for a big lens on a monopod or tripod.

Page27 Semipalmated Plover
Nome, Alaska (June 2001) *Nikon F5, 600 mm f4 with 1.4x TC, Kodak E100 VS*

The Nome trip was my first workshop with Ralph Paonessa, who scouted the off-roads for photo opportunities well before our group convened. In the middle of nowhere (which describes most of the roads near Nome), Ralph came upon a plover nest whose coordinates he locked into his GPS unit. We returned several days later, and the bird was dutifully tending her eggs. She got up when we set up our gear and moved nervously across the rocky terrain. I noticed a tiny patch of Tundra wildflowers, hoping she would pause here as she made her way back to the nest. This is one of the few shots in the book where I used fill-flash with a Better Beamer magnifier to brighten up the overcast scene.

Page28 Surfbirds
Middleton Island, Alaska (July 2000) *Nikon F5, 600 mm f4 lens with 2x TC, Fuji Provia 100*

After a dream shoot with a Bald Eagle nest, I got a second wind and took the long way back to camp, exploring unfamiliar beaches. For the next two hours, I encountered six species of shorebird amidst the boulder-strewn beach. One mixed flock looked promising as I patiently maneuvered into position. I could identify a few Western Sandpipers, but there were some less familiar species mixed in. While working this group, I found a small group of stunning birds that would later be identified as Surfbirds—my first sighting ever. Considering the remoteness of this location, I was surprised that they let me work in this close. Seconds later, a neighboring shorebird issued an alarm call and everyone took wing.

Page29 American Wigeon
Mission Bay, California (January 2003) *Nikon F100, 600 mm f4 lens with 1.4x TC, Kodak E100 VS*

On my first trip to California, I met a wonderful nutritionist and photographer, Dr. Cliff Oliver, who is a friend of Arthur Morris. I sought his counsel on my return trip in 2001 and scheduled an appointment. Invariably, we chatted about birds and he recommended a spot nearby in San Diego for great duck photography. As soon as I pulled into Paradise Point Resort and glanced at the ponds, I was in heaven... loads of wigeon and scaup milling about at close-range. These wild ducks were used to being fed and quite approachable. What makes the shoot especially nice is the lush landscaping around the ponds, which reflect beautiful colors in still water.

Rhapsody In Blue

Page30 Mandarin Duck
Santee Lakes, California (January 2001) *Nikon F5, 600 mm f4 lens with 1.4x TC, Fuji Provia 100*

On our first morning shoot at Santee Lakes with Artie's group, we worked a group of Wood Ducks from the bank tossing out bread. From out of nowhere came a drake Mandarin, one of the most spectacular waterfowl in the entire world. I could hardly believe my eyes, as he mixed in with the other ducks and coots. This species is native to the Far East. Having escaped from private collections in the United States, it is now living wild and breeding in California. After one pass, the Mandarin swam off and I was disappointed that I couldn't get a closer shot. On the third morning, he returned and this time was in camera range for some glorious portraits in soft light.

Page30 Ringed-neck Duck
Soccoro Pond, New Mexico (November 1998) *Nikon F5, 600 mm f4 lens with 1.4x TC, Fuji Sensia 100*

Base camp for my first big shoot at Bosque del Apache was the big town of Soccoro, a few miles north of the famous wildlife refuge. After a productive morning shoot, Artie took our group to a small pond at The New Mexico Institute of Mining & Technology. I was surprised that any wildlife would easily be found in this urban setting. Yet, a few dozen American Wigeon call this pond home each winter. We were having a grand time making flight and preening shots of the wigeon. At one point, I looked up and there was a solitary Ring-necked Duck, definitely one of the more elusive North American waterfowl species to photograph. There was just one instant when he swam directly toward me. I love the effect of a head-on shot, making eye contact.

Page30 Wandering Tattler & Harbor Seals
La Jolla, California (January 2003) *Nikon F5, 600 mm f4 lens, Fuji Provia 100*

After a wonderful morning shoot with pelicans at the La Jolla cliffs, we ventured just a stone's throw away to Children's Beach, which is reserved for harbor seals. Every day there is a different assortment of seals hauled out on the sandy beach. They can be photographed at close range, though walking amidst the seals is no longer permitted. That morning there were at least five species of shorebirds feeding among the lumbering mounds of fur, making for great habitat shots. At first I thought that this bird was a Willet, but something was off. A neighboring photographer confirmed that this was a tattler, a new species for my list. I love it when that happens!

Page31 Greater Flamingo
Great Inagua, Bahamas *Nikon F5, 600 mm f4 lens with 2x TC, Fuji Provia 100*

Pictures of captive flamingoes are so commonplace that one assumes that getting close is easy. I thought that photographing wild ones in the Bahamas would be a snap, but was I wrong on that account. The birds were highly skittish, partially because they live in such a remote and isolated habitat that people do not normally get close in their protected sanctuary. For this shot, I had to wade out into the salt ponds up to my knees, quite a challenge considering that the invisible bottom was very jagged. These birds were far away. Fortunately, the optics are pretty good at 1200 mm with today's lenses. I made the shot at F16 to render as many of the birds in focus as possible.

Page31 Bar-tailed Godwit
Nome, Alaska (June 2001) *Nikon F5, 600 mm f4 lens with 1.4x TC, Kodak E100 VS*

Photographing birds on the tundra is arduous work, hauling heavy equipment over uneven, soggy terrain. Once you find birds, they are likely to move away quickly before you get into camera range. The goal is to find a bird that will stick around because it has a nest somewhere nearby. This Bar-tailed Godwit, a bird that defies the odds by completing a non-stop winter migration to New Zealand, was remarkably tolerant of our group of photographers shooting from only 20 feet away. We went back another day and despite having GPS coordinates on it, we were hard pressed to spot it. This is a true master of disguise, a trait that keeps the marauding foxes and jaegers at bay.

Page32 Little Blue Heron
Estero Lagoon, Florida (December 2000) *Nikon F5, 600 mm f4 lens with 1.4x TC, Kodak E100 VS*

There was one small perch in my favorite lagoon on Fort Myers Beach that wading birds used regularly. Walking along the bank, I noticed a few sculpted pieces of deadwood and decided to create a little reef by adding them to the one already anchored for a series of multiple perches. Once again, Estero Lagoon did not disappoint. The next day, three birds were all perched together on my set-up. This handsome Little Blue Heron was flanked by two Snowy Egrets. After a bird rests for awhile, it may stretch out just like a person would. The key is to anticipate your shots. If you hang out with a bird long enough, it's just a matter of time before it does something interesting.

Page32 Brown Pelican
Bolsa Chica, California (January 1999) *Nikon F5, 400 mm f5.6 Tokina lens, Fuji Sensia 100*

For three glorious days, our instructional photo tour with Artie watched pelicans plunge-dive for fish very close to the footbridge by the main parking lot at Bolsa Chica Ecological Reserve. How easy it is to take things for granted; on two subsequent trips here in January 2001 and 2003, the pelicans never fished anywhere near the bridge, as the baitfish were no longer concentrating here. How lucky we were on that first trip in 1999. Fortunately, I spent most of my time concentrating on the dive sequence both with a 600mm f4 on a monopod and a handheld, lightweight 400mm f5.6 autofocus Tokina lens. For such huge birds, they are surprisingly agile when diving right in front of you.

Page33 Blue-footed Boobies
Isabel Island, Mexico (December 2000) *Nikon N90s, 80-400 mm f4.5 lens, Fuji Velvia 50*

After so many shoots where wild birds were reluctant to being approached, what a joy to photograph nesting seabirds so intimately on this lush tropical island. Unlike boobies at the Galapagos Islands, these Mexican birds have almost no exposure to people, yet they were as docile as could be. The Blue-footed Booby colony sat on the crest of a ridge. Of the nearly 100 pairs that I saw, this particular couple drew me in with dad standing guard as his mate incubated the eggs. By remaining with birds for a while, you get to see interesting behaviors like the head scratch. Do to the vibration reduction feature of my new zoom lens, I could stop down to f11 for added depth-of-field and still make a sharp photo.

Page34 White Ibis
Estero Lagoon, Florida (February 2001) *Nikon F5, 600 mm f4 lens with 1.4x TC, Fuji Provia 100*

The moment that I saw this slide, I knew that it was special, a standout from all the other White Ibis shots that I had taken on other trips to Florida. Quite simply, the interplay of white, blue and orange is very pleasing to the eye. I also like the spike of mangrove that suggests a touch of habitat without being too distracting. Since the plumage of this species is so stark, I wouldn't consider shooting it unless bathed in the soft light of the golden hour. Exposing for a bright white bird would require some thought with my older Nikon models, but the F5's 3D matrix metering handles it like a pro, with no exposure compensation in most situations.

Page35 Cinnamon Teal
Newport Back Bay, California (January 2003) *Nikon F5, 600 mm f4 lens with 2x TC, Kodak E100 VS*

Kristie calls this picture "The Geisha Duck" as it appears to be peering out from behind a fan formed by the preened wing-feathers. Many other ducks were in the vicinity; I was lucky to have a clean view of this single bird. Action sequences like preening are so intricate that it is hard to intentionally capture the absolute peak moment; there is a slight delay from the time that you notice the moment to when the finger fully depresses the shutter release. Chalk it up to serendipity that the duck's red eye is framed by the erect feathers. This was certainly not planned. I was really pushing it with 1200 mm on a monopod at 1/125 of a second, shooting a burst to insure at least one sharp frame.

Page36 Black-necked Stilt
Lake Kissimmee, Florida (April 1999) *Nikon F5, 600 mm f4 lens with 1.4x TC, Kodak E100 VS*

The pristine wetlands that border Lake Kissimmee support a healthy population of stilts, among others. While zooming around in a chartered airboat looking for Snail Kites, I couldn't help but notice these stilts towering on delicate pink legs. This was my only opportunity to show one on land, illustrating just how strange the bird's profile is. I asked the captain to drift by him at close range with the motor off. There was but one ideal moment when the full extension of the legs showed through a gap in the vegetation. With great fortune, he turned his head for the perfect profile as a breeze carried us by his little island. Only because the sun was low does the beautiful eye photograph ruby-red.

Page37 Piping Plover
Assateague Island, Maryland (May 2000) *Nikon F5, 600 mm f4 lens with 1.4x TC, Kodak E100 VS*

This was one of those shoots when many hours of work boil down to a few critical seconds. The north end of Assateague Island hosts a handful of nesting Piping Plovers. During the summer it is closed to the public to help protect this endangered species. I networked with friends and secured permission to tag along with the biologists who were monitoring the nests and installing wire-mesh enclosures to exclude predators. We had visited maybe six nests that day and all of the birds were skittish and remained well out of camera range. My hopes hung on the last nest of the day. This tiny plover was darting all over the place, but for one shining moment, paused amidst some shoots of dune grass.

Photography Notes

Page37 Semipalmated Sandpiper
Jamaica Bay, New York (August 1999) *Nikon F5, 600 mm f4 lens with 1.4x TC, Fuji Velvia 50*

Most people do not realize how much hard work goes into a simple portrait of a sandpiper. Essentially, you need to be on top of these highly skittish birds with a monster lens, the lower the angle of view the better. This peep was maybe 25 feet away. Arthur Morris demonstrated how to get close consistently on this tour. Arthur recommends taking the low road with your belly to the ground. Despite the unpleasantries of mucking around on a mudflat, the real challenge was moving the big camera, pivoting on elbows to drag the body forward, cradling 15 pounds. After all that, the birds might fly off if alarmed. It's better to work a single bird than a group with many eyes watching.

Page37 Least Sandpiper
Bolsa Chica, California (January 2001) *Nikon F5, 600 mm f4 lens with 2x TC, Kodak E100 VS*

Having seen many Least Sandpipers over the prior two years, but never getting close enough to make a shot, I had given up on getting this species for the book. Then one fine day at Bolsa Chica, where there is always something to shoot, I came upon a small pool with two of these peeps feeding. Already close when I spotted them, there was no stalking involved. I simply lowered to the ground and popped on the 2x teleconverter for 1200 mm. This may be the easiest shorebird picture I ever took for the project. The static nature of this portrait belies how frenetic feeding shorebirds are. There were just a few seconds of quick poses. Many blurred sandpiper slides have been tossed in the trash.

Page38 Wood Stork
Everglades National Park, Florida (February 1993) *Nikon F3, 600 mm f4 lens, Fujichrome 100*

This shot was taken several years before the project began during my very first shoot outside of Maryland with a big telephoto lens. A top destination was the famed Mzarek Pond, known for hosting huge feeding sprees. Unfortunately there were only a few birds there, but I was delighted to be able to make full-frame portraits of anything at that point in my career. Normally I wouldn't shoot with strong backlighting, but this was my very first Wood Stork and I couldn't resist. A blessing in disguise, two backlit droplets dripping off the bill make the shot for me. Some people say that you have to take lots of pictures to get a few good ones, but I don't believe art is a function of chance.

Page39 Wood Stork
Sarasota Bay, Florida (February 2001) *Nikon F5, 80-400 mm f4.5 zoom lens, Kodak E100 VS*

On my travels around Florida, I ran into all sorts of bird photographers at all the favorite spots. By and large, this is a very friendly and cooperative group of people. Someone told me of the "Pelican Man" sanctuary on Tavanier Key by Sarasota Bay, and I needed a look for myself. Numerous wild birds mingle here with the captives in rehab. Right next door was a boat ramp popular with local fishermen. When fish are cleaned at the dock, local waterbirds know about it. This lovely juvenile Wood Stork was looking for handouts and therefore quite approachable. I waited until he moved into black water (reflecting a shaded tree) to offset the white plumage for a dramatic portrait.

Page40 Magnificent Frigatebird
Isabel Island, Mexico (December 2000) *Nikon F5, 80-400 mm f4.5 zoom lens, Kodak E100 VS*

Of the many frigatebirds sitting in the short trees on the island, I was drawn to this one because he was the lone juvenile male. Perhaps he was taking notes amidst the breeding area where lots of adults flaunted their red pouches. I angled the shot to frame in a soft green background to complement his striking colors. Of all the shots that I took, this one stood out, bill crooked over the back. Isabel is one of those rare places where nesting birds can be approached at close range without frightening them, probably due to the lack of predators on these remote islands. I was very fortunate to have just purchased the new vibration-reduction 80-400 zoom lens as I used it for most of my shots on the island.

Page41 Doubled-crested Cormorant
Anhinga Trail, Florida (February 2001) *Nikon F5, 200 mm f4 macro lens, Fuji Provia 100*

There's no place like the Anhinga Trail for getting so close to so many beautiful wild birds on a consistent basis. This fellow was only three feet away, perched on the grassy canal bank. I sat down with him for an eye-to-eye meeting. For half an hour, I shot nearly 50 frames, carefully framing the background, a solid wall of blue water. It's critical to avoid distracting background elements (branches, other birds, etc.) that throw off a picture's balance. During the shoot, he was constantly looking in different directions, well aware of the huge gators that patrol the pond. This angle shows off his namesake crest, a feature not regularly displayed.

Page42 Heermann's Gull
La Jolla, California (January 1999) *Nikon F5, 600 mm f4 lens with 1.4x TC, Fuji Velvia 50*

This shot was made at Children's Beach. Once popular with the locals, it's now reserved for a robust colony of harbor seals. Tourists flock here to delight in seals hauled out on the small beach. Upon getting my fill of cute whiskered faces, I walked around and found this gull perched high upon a boulder overlooking the beach. I never pass up an opportunity for a nice clean portrait, especially when complementary colors like red and blue come into play. Initially, I was disappointed that I cut off the feet, but as I recall, the rock was covered with whitewash, which would have been distracting. I'm always fascinating by how a bird can tuck the leg into the body and make it disappear under the feathers.

Page42 Royal Tern
Cape May, New Jersey (October 2000) *Nikon F5, 600 mm f4 lens with 1.4x TC, Kodak E100 VS*

Pictures like this look so simple, but they are quite a challenge to make. The necessary ingredients—an isolated bird, low angle of view, soft light, clean background, an approachable bird—all have to synchronize to make this possible. Like many seabirds, the Royal Tern is social, often roosting in a group with other terns, gulls and skimmers. I search for individuals on the periphery to avoid distracting out-of-focus background birds. This tern was resting on a berm, so all I had to do was kneel down to see him eye-to-eye. The low angle helps to soften the background by making it more distant and out-of-focus. I waited until the head turned sufficiently to catch the soft sidelight.

Page43 Tufted Puffin
Middleton Island, Alaska (July 2000) *Nikon F5, 600 mm f4 lens with 1.4x TC, Kodak E100 VS*

The tent where I was stationed on my namesake island was a short walk from a cliff that hosted a colony of Tufted Puffins. Every time I peered over the edge, the birds below would fly off. Since the nest is a tunnel in the cliff face, there was nothing to see at that point. These guys have little or no contact with people, as only a handful of biologists work here during the breeding season. I learned to slow down my approach and present myself to the birds as gently as possible. This stoic puffin accepted me into his world and treated me to a nice big yawn in addition to some great face-to-face stares. I probably underexposed the frame 1/3 stop, so as not to burn out the white face.

Page44 King Eider
Barrow, Alaska (June 2000) *Nikon F5, 600 mm f4 lens with 1.4x TC, Kodak E100 VS*

When I first saw a picture of a King Eider drake in one of my field guides, I was awestruck at the beauty of the colors and design. Not knowing how to find it in the wild, I initially planned to shoot a zoo bird. As the project unfolded, I was able to get so many tough birds in the wild that I decided everything must be wild. I met a guy in Minnesota who told me that King Eider could be photographed in Barrow on Alaska's North Slope. I booked a trip for the following summer, but did not see a King Eider until the second to last day of the trip. A van of birders pulled over and gave me the location. This lone drake was accepting beyond my wildest dreams and posed for 50 rolls of unforgettable moments.

Page44 Blue-winged Teal
Wakodahatchee Wetlands, Florida (March 1998) *Nikon N90s, 600 mm f4 lens with 1.4 TC, Fuji Velvia 50*

Wakodahatchee Wetlands near Boynton Beach on Florida's Atlantic Coast is a phenomenal venue where lots of beautiful birds are easily accessible from a boardwalk that traverses lush vegetated ponds. This image is all about timing. Normally, a resting teal is a good looking bird, but when the speculum shows, it is extraordinary. This one had just finished preening and flashed its secondary feathers before tucking them into the body. I've also had luck with the Green-winged Teal here, another species that is hard to approach in the wild. Be patient with a great subject and keep your finger on the trigger as special moments tend to be very fleeting.

Page45 Long-tailed Duck
Churchill, Canada (June 1998) *Nikon N90s, 600 mm f4 lens, Fuji Sensia 100*

We saw a number of Long-tailed drakes at Churchill that spooked easily and I had given up hope of such a portrait. Our van with five photographers pulls into a parking lot by a lake, which hosts a pair of loons. This handsome drake was perched just beyond the vehicle and continued to rest calmly on the shore while our group approached with big lenses. My surprise was only surpassed by my delight. After about 10 minutes of clicking away, he decided to move on and swam off at a leisurely pace. I do believe that birds are aware of the difference between a brazen intruder and an appreciative guest. When the energy is right, they bestow wonderful gifts. I try to leave a little extra space on the side that the bird faces.

Page46 Green-winged Teal
Port Aransas, Texas (March 2000) *Nikon N90s, 600 mm f4 lens with 1.4x TC, Fuji Velvia 50*

I heard great things about the Port Aransas Birding Center, so we made a stop there on our tour of the Texas Coast. Within minutes of visiting this place, I could see what all the fuss was about. A small vegetated island next to the boardwalk hosted an assortment of resting ducks, mostly teal and pintail. In most locales, these wary dabblers are unapproachable. Here they are so used to birders that they don't even bat an eye when you walk past from 20 feet away. For just a moment, this resting Green-winged Teal hen displayed her brilliant green speculum. Two other species of teal were right under my nose along with a dozen Northern Pintail.

Page46 American Wigeon
Homeland Lakes, Maryland (January 2000) *Nikon F5, 600 mm f4 lens with 1.4x TC, Kodak E100 VS*

The Baltimore neighborhood where I grew up is well known for its five lovely ponds where families stroll with their children and feed the resident Mallards. One day I was passing through and decided to stop to feed the ducks, as I had a 50 lb. bag of corn. Two birds stood out in the crowd, a pair of American Wigeon, which really surprised me for such an urban setting. I returned the next day with my camera and fortunately they were still there. Although the hen lacks the male's iridescent green, I love her markings and warm earth tones. I've photographed many a hen wigeon at premier North American venues, but this is my favorite portrait, taken where I used to skip stones as a kid.

Page47 Ring-necked Duck
Santee Lakes, California (January 2001) *Nikon F5, 600 mm f4 lens with 1.4x TC, Kodak E100 VS*

I've only had the pleasure of photographing wild Ring-necked Ducks on three occasions during the five years of shooting for this project. They tend to be encountered in very small groups and are highly suspicious of any focused attention. Santee Lakes was added as a stop on Arthur Morris' Southern California photography tour. Within an hour's drive of San Diego, the lakes host a great variety of ducks that are accustomed to people. Nearly a dozen species willingly take handouts from the locals. I selected this image for the sweet blues in the rippling water. I'm always amazed how birds can fold their wings into their bodies to perfectly match the contour.

Page47 Northern Pintail
Paradise Point Resort, California (January 2001) *Nikon F5, 600 mm f4 lens with 1.4x TC, Kodak E100 VS*

A friend of Artie's from San Diego, Cliff Oliver, an outstanding nature photographer, was kind enough to tell us about a fabulous venue for wintering ducks on Mission Bay. Two of my favorites, wigeon and pintail are regulars at Paradise Point Resort. The wild birds are utterly tame as long as you approach them respectfully. The backgrounds are superb with lush landscaping reflecting in the water. I waited for this hen pintail to move into this spot of painterly reflections. When I returned to San Diego two years later, we stayed at Paradise Point and all of our feathered friends were still there in addition to a lone wild Mandarin hen.

Page48 Pacific Loon
Churchill, Canada (June 1998) *Nikon F5, 600 mm f4 lens with 2x TC, Fujichrome 100*

More than any other, this gorgeous species of loon was my motivation for traveling to Churchill. How can you not be mesmerized by the lavender velvet that adorns the head? I thought that this shot would be easy, having seen many published images of Pacific Loons from Churchill. At the outset of this project, I had no idea how tough shots like this would be. Several days passed before we had decent light to warrant attempting a shot of a known nest near town. It was bitter cold and our tour leader allowed no more than a few precious minutes to photograph the bird if she got off the nest, which she did when we were about 75 feet away. I popped on the 2x and fired away.

Page49 Western Grebe
Freezeout Lake, Montana (June 1999) *Nikon F5, 600 mm f4 lens with 1.4x TC, Kodak E100 VS*

The story of this image starts out in a Home Depot in Baltimore and a lumber yard in Missoula, Montana. I purchased supplies for a rudimentary floating blind that I designed at home with common sense and a large dose of blind faith. My simulated muskrat lodge survived her maiden voyage on Freezeout Lake, where a large colony of grebes nested. The lake is surprisingly shallow, but the soft pungent bottom will swallow up your legs mid-thigh if you are not careful. I saw a momentary head-on glare one day from a Western Grebe, but missed the shot and hoped for another chance. Two days later, it happened at close-range and my finger was on the trigger. A good title is "Catching the Red Eye."

Page50 Northern Harrier
Aberdeen Proving Ground, Maryland (February 1997) *Nikon F3, 600 mm f4 lens with 1.4x TC, Kodak 100 LPZ*

By the grace of God, I was permitted to photograph the wildlife at APG, an army post in my home state. A fellow on the environmental unit escorted me around the area's prime habitat bordering the Chesapeake Bay. We saw a lone harrier scouring the fields and I formulated a plan. A photo blind was installed, overlooking a favored field where caged mice were placed underneath a beautiful perch. The first day a harrier scanned the mice briefly, but did not perch and no shots were made. The second day, it landed after a few hours, but I only got off three shots before the raptor lost interest and took off. Perhaps the camera clicks were too much for this wary hunter.

Page51 Northern Harrier
Bodega Bay, California (January 1999) *Nikon N90s, 600 mm f4 lens with 1.4x TC, Fuji RMS*

The alluring Grey Ghost... I had been drooling over field guide photos wondering if I would ever get my chance. It was a cold dreary day in the quaint seaside village of Bodega Bay north of San Francisco. I was driving back to the hotel after watching some oystercatchers when an unusual bird in the marsh caught my attention. I circled around to the parking lot and rigged up, not knowing what I had. I approached cautiously using a road sign to block the bird's view of me. I stepped to the side and revealed myself while focusing on my prize. I couldn't believe it—a male harrier. Trembling with excitement, I got about 5 seconds of shooting before he flew off. The bird probably knew what I was up to all along.

Page52, 53 Bald Eagles
Homer, Alaska (March 2003) *Nikon F5, 600 mm f4 lens with 1.4x TC, Fuji Velvia 50*

Making tight portraits of wild Bald Eagles is highly probable in the magical little world that is the Eagle Lady's backyard in Homer. Jean has been feeding eagles daily in the winter for nearly two decades. During my first visit in January 1999, we only had one day of blue sky and I wanted to go back to take advantage of the wonderful opportunity. The adult bird on the left was perched on her tool shed maybe 10 feet off the ground. No matter how many times I photograph eagles, it is always a thrill as they are so regal and inspiring. The group of four immature eagles was also perched on top of a shed. I stopped down my aperture to f16 to maximize depth of field, still very small with a big lens.

Page54 Cattle Egret
St. Augustine, Florida (April 1998) *Nikon F5, 600 mm f4 lens with 1.4x TC, Fuji Provia 100*

Bird photographers flock to the alligator farm in St. Augustine during the spring nesting season when five or six species of wading birds can be easily viewed. Bob and I nicknamed this bird "Firebill" since it was the most intensely colored Cattle Egret in the colony. At other times of the year, the legs and bill would be yellow, but surging hormones of breeding translate into a stunning beauty. Firebill postured in a number of trees, but this cypress perch offered a clean, green background. In this moment of high spirits, the crest is raised. Curiously, the Cattle Egret is an immigrant from Africa, having spread throughout much of North America's southern latitudes in the past century.

Page55 Tricolored Heron
St. Augustine, Florida (April 2001) *Nikon F100, 80-400 mm f4.5 zoom lens, Kodak E100 VS*

The breeding Tricolored Heron is nothing short of a knockout. No wonder it was one of John James Audubon's favorites. This individual was only ten feet away from the boardwalk at the big alligator pond, strutting his stuff to attract a mate to his tree of choice. Once I find a special bird, I may work with it for hours. This heron commanded several rolls of film, primarily because I was able to isolate him against a clean background. Many of the birds here perch in tangles of branches that are very distracting. Because so many photographers and visitors crowd the boardwalk, it's best to arrive early in the morning.

Page56 Great Blue Heron
Sarasota Bay, Florida (December 2000) *Nikon F5, 600 mm f4 with 1.4x TC, Kodak E100 VS*

I learned from Artie that fishing docks in Florida are a great place to photograph watebirds. The easiest way to get a meal is to let a fisherman toss you scraps upon filleting the catch-of-the-day. I found this particular dock just by exploring on a day set aside for surprises. Pelicans and gulls are notorious freeloaders, but some wading birds invariably take note of the possibilities. Since these birds are so approachable, super-tight shots are very possible. I worked this Great Blue Heron for over two hours as he moved around the dock jockeying for position. The yawn helps to illustrate the sharpness of the bill. Quick reflexes are necessary to capture such a fleeting moment.

Photography Notes

Page56 Great Egret
St. Augustine, Florida (April 2001) *Nikon F100, 600 mm f4, Kodak E100 VS*

The administration of The St. Augustine Alligator Farm has been very understanding of photographers that visit the rookery. Like others, I have been able to call ahead and gain access to the rookery when staff arrive a few hours before the gates open to the public. Thus, we can capitalize on the beautiful morning light. This bird drew me in with its luxurious courtship plumes swaying in the breeze. For most of the shoot, this Great Egret had his head turned a bit towards me, losing the light on his face and bill. I waited until he angled such that the rays would illuminate the head. The shaded vegetation in the background went completely black when exposing for the white bird.

Page57 Great White Heron
Sanibel Island, Florida March 1999) *Nikon F5, 600 mm f4 with 1.4x TC, Fuji Velvia 50*

I heard about a very tolerant Great White Heron that frequented the pass between Sanibel and Captiva Island, so I checked it out on my next trip to Florida. Sure enough, he was fishing near the beach and we approached with great caution. An hour later, we were shooting eyeball shots; this guy loved us. Just before sunset, he walked onto the beach and strolled a bit before resting in a grassy area. That soft glow of the golden hour was in effect. I positioned myself such that a shaded area was the background. Note this bird's whitish legs; the look-alike Great Egret has black legs and stands a bit shorter than this rare color morph of the Great Blue Heron, found in southern Florida.

Page58 White-cheeked Pintail
Pericles' Pond, The Bahamas (May 2000) *Nikon F5, 600 mm f4 lens, Fuji Provia 100*

Friends of my parents lived in the Bahamas and were very involved with the local birding community. Hearing about the project, they kindly hooked me up with the right people. Before flying to Great Inagua to see the wild flamingos, I hoped to see the "Bahama Pintail," as it is known. A name was given to me of someone who fed wild ducks at his home and I received an invitation. Several ponds on his estate were loaded with pintails eagerly awaiting the daily feeding. I shot about fifteen rolls of these stunning waterfowl as they were very tolerant and quite animated. This shot is one of my favorites as the birds juxtaposed so well. The males and females are look-alikes, unusual for ducks.

Page58 Common Moorhen
Venice, Florida (February 2001) *Nikon F5, 600 mm f4 lens with 2x TC, Fuji Velvia 50*

Moorhens were not an expected subject that morning at the Venice Rookery where photographers congregate to document the drama of nesting herons. The pond is known to have big alligators. I was a bit surprised to see a pair of moorhens swimming across the pond at a leisurely pace. Shooting on a tripod with a Wimberley head, I swung the camera to them and snapped two or three frames before the birds separated. Opportunities for a synchronized pair shot are few and far between, so I was grateful for the moment. Autofocus is not supposed to work with a 2x teleconverter, but sometimes it saves the day.

Page59 Mute Swans
Magothy River, Maryland (February 2003) *Nikon F5, 600 mm f4 lens with 1.4x TC, Kodak E100 VS*

I have visited this private dock many times as there are always waterfowl hanging out for the daily feeding of hard corn. The owner of the property kindly lets me throw out corn when he's not around. Mute Swans mate for life and stay together through the year. I love the heart shape formed by their sinuous necks and bills, symbolizing their bond. If there was a video clip of this particular scene, you would see the two birds constantly moving, albeit slowly as they went about their business. That's why it's so important to keep your eye in the viewfinder and your finger on the trigger. These peak moments are so fleeting.

Page60 American Bittern
Anhinga Trail, Florida (March 1999) *Nikon F5, 600 mm f4 lens with 1.4 TC, Fuji Velvia 50*

This image reminds me why I love the Anhinga Trail in Everglades National Park. I've only photographed wild American Bitterns five times in my career. They are notoriously shy birds. For three mornings in a row, this bird was hanging in the same spot and he gave us many good looks admidst the dense cover. I started out taking really tight shots at 1200 mm, but decided to pull back and show a little more habitat, appropriate for a bird who needs surrounding vegetation to feel at home. At one point, the bittern fed next to the trail to the delight of a dozen photographers. I pushed my film one stop throughout the prodject for extra shutter speed and depth of field.

Page61 Least Bittern
Wakulla Springs, Florida (January 2000) *Nikon F5, 600 mm f4 lens with 1.4x TC, Kodak E100 VS*

This was one of the coldest shoots of the project... in Florida of all places! A rogue cold spell had blanketed the Deep South and it felt like it would snow. Despite having packed a pair of glove liners, I had to pocket my hands every few minutes to bring my numb digits back to life. The birds at Wakulla Springs are used to pontoon boats parading tourists through the beautiful cypress swamp. I hired my own boat to allow time for working great subjects. We were right on top of this shy female as the boat drifted by. There was just a moment for a clean look at the bird hiding in the reeds. A moment later, she retreated into the marsh. That's about all you can hope for with the bitterns.

Page61 Clapper Rail
Palo Alto Baylands, California (January 1999) *Nikon N90s, 600 mm f4 lens, Fuji RMS (400)*

I heard through the grapevine that the best chance for seeing the elusive California Clapper Rail was from the boardwalk at the Baylands nature center in Palo Alto just south of San Francisco. The one day that we were in the area, I checked it out. Sure enough, a movement in the reeds turned out to be the rail. Under the best of circumstances, rail photography is tough work as they are extremely reclusive and camouflage well. Remarkably, I was able to make some full-body shots of this Clapper Rail, but preferred this frame since it illustrates how a rail normally appears—a phantom in the marsh. Four years later, I walked the same boardwalk and never saw a bird.

Page62 Northern Jacana
San Crisobal River, Mexico (December 2000) *Nikon F5, 600 mm f4 lens with 1.4x TC, Kodak E100 VS*

I hired a jungle boat guide to tour us around the lush San Cristobal River in San Blas, hoping to find the Boat-billed Heron, Bare-throated Tiger Heron and Northern Jacana... a tall order for one boat ride. After searching a mile or two of heavily vegetated river, we came upon an open marshy area that looked promising for the jacana. The first bird seen was a tiger heron—a real rarity. However, he flew away when I called out with excessive enthusiasm and I felt like a fool. Around the bend, the jacana made his appearance. We worked him for an hour as he hopped across lily pads in search of food. The underside of the wings is bright yellow, but I never saw a wing flap.

Page63 Purple Gallinule
Wakodahatchee Wetlands, Florida (March 1998) *Nikon N90s 600 mm f4 lens, Fuji Velvia 50*

On the inaugural Florida trip that inspired this book, I met a photographer, Bill Smiley, at the Venice Rookery. I mentioned the Purple Gallinule as a target species and he told me about Wakodahatchee Wetlands near Boynton Beach. The itinerary was altered a bit to accommodate this good tip. Bob Rinker found this gallinule and called me in with his walkie-talkie. The plant that the bird was working looked Amazonian, standing nearly five feet out of the water with goliath leaves. Birds are quite acclimated here and the gallinule paid us no attention while foraging on the seed pods. All this good fortune resulted from a conversation, reaching out to a stranger.

Page64 Limpkin
Myakka River, Florida (February 2001) *Nikon F5, 600 mm f4 lens, Kodak E100 VS*

Myakka River State Park is a well-known venue for seeing Sandhill Cranes and the Limpkin. In 1998, we traveled here with high hopes only to find that the main area was closed due to flooding of the roads. On this visit in 2001, fortune was on our side and we found a Limpkin just below the dam at the big lake. The Limpkin is a very hard bird to find, so I took full advantage of this gorgeous individual foraging in a lush setting. If you stay with a bird long enough, you are likely to get unusual postures and key moments like this yawn that makes the picture stand out in a crowd. The species is known for its booming call, so this portrait with an open bill seems appropriate.

Page64 Pie-billed Grebe
Wakodahatchee Wetlands, Florida (March 1999) *Nikon N90s, 600 mm f4 lens with 1.4x TC, Fuji Sensia 100*

I've always found the Pie-billed Grebe to be endearing and welcome a good opportunity with this shy bird. I was cruising the boardwalk and out of nowhere this grebe showed up and gave me a dynamite series of poses. Two months prior, I found one stranded on a beach in San Diego. It looked fine, but circling gulls indicated that it was in trouble. I borrowed a cell phone and tracked down a vet on Super Bowl Sunday who would take it provided that I drive it to him. Despite being on a group shoot, I felt compelled to help out and made the run, cradling the frightened grebe as a friend drove the car. I like to think that the Florida grebe gave me a gift for helping out his brother from California.

Rhapsody In Blue

Page65 Belted Kingfisher
Druid Hill Park, Maryland (November 2001) *Nikon F5, 600 mm f4 lens with 2x TC, Fuji Provia 100*

My second incarnation of a floating blind was built to get close to Hooded Mergansers that visit a secluded lake at the Baltimore Zoo each fall. Brimming with confidence from my shoot with grebes in Montana, I thought that I would get right on top of the hoodies with my new-and-improved blind. I didn't fool any of these wary little ducks. Alas, a kingfisher began to hunt. To my astonishment, I was able to swim over without even a flinch from this famously shy bird. He ate a minnow on this snag, but I missed it. Undeterred, I prefocused on the perch and waited for an hour... an eternity when your chest waders have flooded with cold November pond water. History did repeat itself!

Page66 Pacific Golden-Plover
Nome, Alaska (June 2001) *Nikon F5, 600 mm f4 lens with 2x TC, Kodak E100 VS*

Several days into my Nome trip, I had serious doubts about doing justice to the lovely Pacific Golden-Plover. Our group of five found several on the tundra, but they would always lead us on a wild goose chase out of camera range. Another pair was found in a prime area near town. With lots of patience, we were able to pinpoint the nest. During our first shoot here, the female incubated the nest while the male stayed off in the distance. The next day, I returned while the group worked another area. This time, the male actually came in and incubated the nest. I think he was more comfortable with a single photographer and I was able to get very close.

Page66 Wilson's Plover
Estero Lagoon, Florida (March 1999) *Nikon N90s, 600 mm f4 lens with 1.4x TC, Fuji Provia 100*

On my way back from yet another fantastic afternoon of shooting at Estero, I noticed a group of sandpipers feeding on mudflats loaded with nutrients from the receding tide. One plump fellow caught my attention—it was a Wilson's Plover, a new bird for me. Shorebirds in a group have to be approached with great caution as they all fly off if just one bird gets spooked and sounds the alarm for all. When plovers feed, they do a lot of running, so autofocus really helps out. Once he knew that I was onto him, keeping close was an exercise in futility. Birds choose when you get to take pictures, and they let you know when the shoot is over.

Page67 Wilson's Phalarope
Freezeout Lake, Montana (June 1999) *Nikon F5, 600 f4 lens with 1.4x TC, Fuji RMS (200)*

After a successful day of shooting grebes from my floating blind, I was navigating toward the launch site where a group of shorebirds had congregated. I watched this phalarope feeding for a while and was eager to make a shot. The blind was getting stuck in the shallow muck, as were my legs, so I had to wait for the bird to come to me. Fortunately, he came to the edge of a floating mat of vegetation and I got the reflection that I was hoping for. My camera was only about a foot above the waterline, a very effective angle of view with such a small bird. Fortunately, I packed a lot of film that day and some of my best shots were made on that precious last roll.

Page67 Red Phalarope
Barrow, Alaska (June 2000) *Nikon F5, 600 f4 lens with 1.4x TC, Kodak E100 VS*

This is a very expensive bird to photograph in the wild since you have to travel to the northern rim of the continent. Once you complete the arduous trip to Barrow, they are a common site on the tundra. I was more interested in the more brightly colored of the pair, the female, very unusual for birds. Barrow is quite remote and this bird has probably never seen people before, but she was quite tolerant of my approach. When working birds on the tundra grass, a precise angle is necessary for getting the best balance of the subject in the vegetation. Hip waders are highly recommended on the soggy terrain as feet can get sucked into the soft, thawed muck. On the second day I almost lost my big lense upon falling in a tundra pool.

Page68 Blue-footed Boobies & Frigatebirds
Isabel Island, Mexico (December 2000) *Nikon N90s, 28-200 mm f4 zoom lens, Kodak E100 VS*

Imagine waking up at first light to a sky full of swirling seabirds—frigatebirds, boobies, pelicans, gulls, and tropicbirds. Such was my visit to this Mexican sanctuary for four glorious days. I planned this shot carefully, hiking up a ridge to compress soaring birds against the sunrise with a bit of the island in the corner. There was just enough cloud cover to diffuse the sun to avoid distracting glare on the lens. The birds were moving in and out of the frame quickly, so I fired off a series of images to ensure at least one picture with properly balanced birds. The frigatebirds have crooked wings while the boobies are straight across.

Page69 Bald Eagle
Homer, Alaska (March 2003) *Nikon F5, 300mm f4 lens, Kodak E100 VS*

One of the major reasons that I returned to Homer in March 2003 was that during the first shoot in 1999, we only had blue skies on one day of our stay. Fortunately, this March trip featured clear skies on all but the first day, which meant plenty of flight shots. When the Eagle Lady of Homer starts her feeding sessions in mid-morning, birds pour in from all directions to converge on her small yard. Normally, eagle flight shots would be done with 840mm, but here in Homer the birds are very close if you get an invitation to the yard. A special shot like this results from shooting dozens of landing sequences when birds perch on trees in her yard to eat their gifted fish.

Page70 Northern Gannet
Cape St. Mary's, Newfoundland (July 1999) *Nikon F5, 600 mm f4 lens, Fuji Velvia 50*

Every once in a while, a giant gannet would soar right below my lofty perch on the cliff. It's very moving to see such a dramatic wingspan amidst a flurry of the much smaller kittiwakes. This bird instantly caught my eye, a sub-adult with dark speckling across the back. Shooting on a monopod really comes in handy in a situation like this one, as I can pan across a wide zone without tripping over tripod legs. With flight photography, it's important for the autofocus sensors to lock onto the subject early before you start accelerated panning to keep the bird centered. Once engaged, Dynamic Autofocus can track a bullet, or so it would seem, as this lens handles speedy ducks well.

Page71 Tufted Puffin
Middleton Island, Alaska (July 2000) *Nikon F5, 600 mm f4 lens with 1.4x TC, Kodak E100 VS*

I was determined to make an interesting flight shot of a puffin after having tried unsuccessfully two years prior in the Pribilofs. A cliff near my tent was the ideal place to try as numerous burrows in the soil underneath meant that birds would be flying right to me. I must have shot fifty sequences of these speed demons, which are so hard to track. Of all the frames I made, this was the only one where the bird seemed to be flying directly at the camera. I especially liked this spot because of the green background, unusual for seabirds nesting on cliffs overlooking water. The huge Alaska earthquake of 1964 lifted part of the seafloor to form land, which greened over as plants took root.

Page71 Northern Fulmar
Pribilof Islands, Alaska (July 1998) *Nikon F5, Tokina 400 mm f4.5 lens, Fuji RA 100*

The Pribilof Islands offer outstanding flight shots of seabirds approaching the cliff faces where they nest. Unlike puffins, auklets and murres, fulmars are relatively slow fliers, comparable to a gull. Normally, I would use my 600 mm lens on a monopod, but these fulmars were close enough and big enough to warrant a handheld flight lens. Frequently, they would make big loops, passing close to the cliff only to swing back out to sea... flying for the pure joy of it, I speculate. This species comes in a light and a dark phase. Both images are cropped horizontals. Vertical flight shooting with a handheld camera feels very awkward to me, so I stick to what feels comfortable.

Page71 Arctic Tern
Nome, Alaska (June 2001) *Nikon F5, 600 mm f4 lens, Fuji Provia 100*

On the one day in eight that we saw blue sky in Nome, I could only think about flight shooting, as white skies don't work well as a background. We returned to a prime section of tundra just past town that hosted a variety of nesters including several pairs of Arctic Tern. Unlike shorebirds, terns will dive-bomb you if you get too close to the nest. Great care must be taken when walking on the tundra loaded with well-camouflaged eggs. A strong ocean breeze enabled the terns to float right above us. I picked this frame for the emphasis on the beautiful forked tail and the head pointing down toward the precious eggs nestled in a clump of grass. GPS technology was very useful for re-visiting cryptic nests.

Page72, 73 Willet & Marbled Godwit
Chula Vista, California (January 2001) *Nikon F5, 600 mm f4 lens, Fuji Provia 100*

Our caravan of eight photographers made an early morning run to Chula Vista, a large estuary south of San Diego with very limited access. Artie knew of a special spot where resting birds at high tide would be within range of a long telephoto lens. Parking by an abandoned shed, we turned the corner to behold a wonderful mixed flock of shorebirds bathed in the first light of morning. The flock consisted mostly of Willets, Marbled Godwits and Short-billed Dowitchers. Small groups of birds would take off on a whim while others would join in. Fast reflexes are required to track a landing shorebird, even with these larger species. I love the Willet's white bands on the underwings.

Page73 Ruddy Turnstone
Sanibel Island, Florida (March 1999) *Nikon F5, 600 mm f4 lens with 1.4x TC, Fuji Provia 100*

Landing in Ft. Myers in the afternoon with about two hours of light left, we made a beeline for the Sanibel-Captiva Bridge. There has never been a shortage of birds in this area where the sea cuts a channel between the two islands. While photographing pelicans diving into the surf, I noticed a Snowy Egret glowing in golden-hour light. Working this bird for a bit, I then saw a lone Ruddy Turnstone taking a bath. Since close-ups of shorebirds are always a challenge, my lens quickly turned to my best opportunity. Within moments, the turnstone jumped up to flap its wings, creating the look of a flight shot. What a great way to start off our second Florida marathon.

Page77 Lesser Scaup
Lake Merritt, California (January 2003) *Nikon F5, 600 mm f4 lens with 1.4x TC, Kodak E100 VS*

While in La Jolla, I overheard a conversation about diving ducks in Oakland. My interest piqued as we would be visiting San Francisco. I introduced myself to the photographers and inquired. Steve recounted how Lake Merritt is a great venue for divers, including both species of goldeneye. Since wild goldeneyes are very elusive, I knew that I had to make a visit while staying in San Francisco. The ducks are quite acclimated to people in this popular urban park, where they are fed daily. While the goldeneyes kept a distance, the scaup were willing subjects. I asked Kristie to throw out some corn to bait the goldeneyes, but it was the Lesser Scaup that splash-landed for the treats.

Page79 Sandhill Cranes & Snow Geese
Bosque del Apache, New Mexico (November 2000) *Nikon F100, 80-400 f4.5 zoom lens, Kodak E100 VS*

We heard of a Great Horned Owl that had been spotted roosting in a thicket near a canal on the wildlife drive. After a bit of searching, his outline was visible in a tangle of branches, making for some nice habitat shots. At the same time, beautiful mist was arising from the adjacent canal, home to a few Pie-billed Grebes. The scene was so ethereal that I really wanted to do it justice. At sunrise, flocks of cranes and geese are constantly moving across the wetlands. Hoping to fill out the composition with some waterfowl, I framed a vertical shot with lots of sky and waited for rows of birds to move across. At Bosque, you don't have to wait too long!

Page81 Brown Pelican
Sarasota Bay, Florida (December 2000) *Nikon F5, 600mm f4 lens, Kodak E100 VS*

Popular marinas in Florida make ideal sites for pelican photography. The birds are so enthralled with the possibility of a free meal that they have little concern for people nearby. At the very instant a fisherman cleaning his catch would lift an arm, as if to toss out the guts, all the pelicans lift their giant bills. It reminds me of a conductor leading his orchestra, without a cue missed. I pre-focused on this lovely juvenile pelican and waited for liftoff once the fish scrap was discarded. This bird was on the periphery of the group where the water was calmer, adding a nice reflection. It helps to leave extra room in a composition to accommodate action like wings spreading.

Page74 Sanderlings
Estero Lagoon, Florida (January 2000) *Nikon F5, 600 mm f4 lens with 1.4x TC, Fuji Provia 100*

While working various species at the far end of the lagoon, I noticed a flock of Sanderlings getting spooked several times. They would take off en mass and zig-zag over the water before returning to roughly the same area. A flock of shorebirds moving as one, twisting and turning with total synchronicity is truly a site to behold. What a golden opportunity should they fly off again, I thought. My patience was rewarded when they lifted off and flew across the beach to open water, filling the frame. Autofocus can get confused with lots of moving birds and may focus out to the background. Here I got lucky. I cannot imagine attempting such a shot just a few years ago before the advent of autofocus.

Page78 Black Skimmers
Cape May, New Jersey (October 2000) *Nikon F5, 600 mm f4 lens, Fuji Provia 100*

Large flocks of skimmers congregate on the main beach at Cape May each fall once the nesting season ends. Resting flocks take wing every so often, whether accidentally scared by beachcombers or as part of their daily movements. Our group of Arthur Morris disciples positioned for a huge liftoff just before sunset. I pondered whether to freeze the action or to attempt a slow shutter speed pan for an artsy effect. With dim light, I opted for the blurred shot and panned at a speed of approximately 1/15 of a second. Of the whole sequence only this frame had the right balance of wispy motion yet definable subjects. I'm glad I opted for the challenge instead of the sure thing.

Page80 Brown Pelican
Bolsa Chica, California (January 1999) *Nikon F5, 600mm f4 lens, Fuji Velvia 50*

My first trip to Southern California was pure bliss, in large part due to the relentless Brown Pelicans that splashed in Bolsa Chica's lagoon. At times, they were too close to bring into focus, dive-bombing baitfish hiding under the footbridge. Most of the time, I used a hand-held 400 mm telephoto to avoid clipping the wings. My 600mm lens on a monopod is a very flexible system, which I used for this shot. After a dive, birds drain the pouch for fish and spring into flight for another attack. I selected this shot as it features the dramatic red pouch of this breeding-plumage adult. In January 2001 and 2003, I returned to Bolsa Chica, but no pelicans were diving. I am so glad that I shot up a storm in 1999.

Page82 White Ibis
Estero Lagoon, Florida (March 1999) *Nikon F5, 600mm f4 lens with 1.4x TC, Kodak E100 VS*

In my limited birding travels, I have found Estero Lagoon at Ft. Myers to be an ideal place to photograph White Ibis. Of the fifteen days spent there on five different trips, there have always been at least a couple ibis feeding in the lagoon. By wearing an old pair of sneakers for wading in the shallows you can get very close . I was walking along the bank with my monopod resting on my shoulder when I saw this bird approaching. Within a couple of seconds, I had autofocus locked on him in sweet morning light. I try to stop shooting once a bird is no longer flying towards me as shots of a rear moving away from the viewer are not as engaging. Of course, there is an exception to every rule, especially when it comes to art.

Page76 Northern Pintail
Bolsa Chica, California (January 2001) *Nikon F5, 600 mm f4 lens with 1.4x TC, Kodak E100 VS*

The plan this morning was to silhouette cormorants against the bright morning sky. Once the sun rose, it was too bright for backlit flight shots as there was no haze on the horizon to diffuse the sun. Nonetheless, I noticed that the lagoon's water was reflecting color well and I keyed in on some pintails frolicking by the footbridge. In the blink of an eye, a drake sprung into flight as I managed to squeeze off a few frames. It happened so quickly that I didn't know if autofocus locked on time. When I got the slides back, I was delighted to see the backlit splash, a moment so fleeting that it doesn't register in real time. The curled tail feather is a nice bonus, helping to identify its owner.

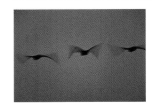

Page78 Double-crested Cormorants
Bolsa Chica, California (January 2001) *Nikon F5, 600 mm f4 lens, Fuji Provia 100*

As sunrise approaches cormorants, ducks and shorebirds start their workday, moving across the main channel at Bolsa Chica. The footbridge by the parking lot gives you a front row seat to all the action, birds steaming head-on against a pastel sky on clear mornings. Artie had the group in position at least half an hour before sunrise to take advantage of the fleeting opportunity. Small bands of cormorants passed overhead every few minutes. The best shutter speed I could manage was 1/8 of a second with the aperture wide open. I selected this image as the motoring of the wings is visible while the bird's outline is clear. Most motion images miss the mark, but reward follows persistence with clear intention.

Page81 American White Pelicans
Freezeout Lake, Montana (June 1999) *Nikon F5, 600mm f4 lens with 1.4x TC, Kodak E100 VS*

While cruising around Freezeout Lake in search of nesting grebes, I periodically peered out of the portholes in my floating blind to see if anything was flying by. Besides grebes, a great variety of waterbirds nest in the area and there's always opportunity for the unexpected. On one occasion, I saw this squadron of pelicans cruising by and managed to shoot three frames with autofocus engaged. I love the layered background... water, reeds, foothills and snow-capped mountains, the way the wings were frozen, the alignment of the birds, the balanced composition—it was all happenstance. The key is to put yourself in a good setting and just let God do all of the magic.

Page83, 84 Great & Snowy Egret
Merritt Island, Florida (April 1999) *Nikon F5, 600mm f4 lens, Fuji Provia 100*

These images were taken on the same morning along the wildlife drive at Merritt Island NWR, just across from the Kennedy Space Center. Wading birds start fishing at first light and may feed in close proximity to one another. I try to stake out a good area and document the comings and goings. I have photographed many Great Egrets in flight, especially at the Venice Rookery. However, no two shots ever look the same, so I keep shooting good opportunities. I was drawn to this Great Egret's bright green lore. A short distance away this Snowy Egret was dipping for minnows in deeper water. He flew back and forth over the same spot and I kept shooting to get that special wing alignment.

Rhapsody In Blue

Page84, 85 Heermann's & Ringed-billed Gull
Coronado Beach, California (January 2001) *Nikon F5, 300mm f4 lens, Kodak E100 VS*

These two images were taken just minutes apart during an Arthur Morris photo tour of Southern California. The wide beach near the famous Hotel del Coronado is a great venue for flight shots of gulls, provided that you're willing to invest in a loaf of bread. The key to a great shoot besides a crisp blue sky is that the sun and the wind are from the same direction. Birds flying into the wind are front-lit and traveling at a far slower speed than with a tailwind. On this particular shoot, the breeze was strong and the gulls were virtually hovering at our fingertips, about the best you can hope for with flight photography. It helps to bring along a designated bread-thrower.

Page84 Bonaparte's Gull
St. Mark's NWR, Florida (January 2000) *Nikon F5, 600mm f4 lens with 1.4x TC, Fuji Provia 100*

My visit to St. Mark's NWR during a January cold spell provided glimpses of lots of good birds, but I couldn't get close to much here. Very few birders were milling about; perhaps the birds are not as acclimated as in classic Florida hotspots. One fine exception was this curious little gull feeding near the road. I had never seen a gull hover and dive for minnows like a tern, so I knew that I had a new bird for my list. For two hours I watched as it made numerous attempts to catch fish. I was equally determined to make something of this opportunity, though it was tough to keep him in the frame. This is a fast, highly maneuverable gull and the camera's autofocus did not like my sudden jerky movements.

Page85 Western Gull
Monterey, California (January 1999) *Nikon N90s, 28-200mm f4.5 zoom lens, Fuji Sensia 100*

Our visit to 17-Mile Drive featured ominous skies with waves crashing across the rocky shoreline. We pulled over at a turnout patrolled by a band of Western Gulls accustomed to working over the tourists for handouts. Ground squirrels also know this drill. Upon making some wide angle scenics, I hoped for a close-up shot of an individual gull in flight. The fading light necessitated fill-flash, which can be very effective with slow shutter speeds in creating a ghosting effect. I rarely shoot autofocus with my short zoom as it is very slow. However, it was my only option and fortunately one or two frames turned out. You don't know the exact wing contortion at the precise moment of exposure since it happens so fast.

Page86 Blue-footed Booby
Isabel Island, Mexico (December 2000) *Nikon NF5, 300mm f4 lens, Kodak E100 VS*

Just before my big Mexico adventure, I purchased a hand-held 300 mm telephoto lens for flight shots in tight quarters. At the top of a bluff sat a Blue-footed Booby colony that I hiked to with great anticipation. What dramatic landings these goofy birds make, huge blue feet braced for impact. Birds would approach from below the cliff from out-of-sight and pop up with no warning. I had about two seconds to find the bird and get the lens centered on him. Maybe twenty sequences were documented that morning with the hopes of at least one decent shot. It all happens so quickly that you don't know what you have until the film is developed. When I saw this image, it was like Christmas morning under the tree!

Page87 American Flamingos
Great Inagua, Bahamas (May 2000) *Nikon NF5, 600mm f4 lens with 1.4x TC, Fuji Provia 100*

This image is a composite of two adjacent frames showing the upstroke and downstroke of the same bird photographed an instant apart. This was a very memorable shoot since I had to wade out into a vast salt lake perhaps 100 yards to get in range of a couple of feeding flamingoes. The bottom was jagged and invisible, necessitating that every step be taken with great care to avoid a fall. Salt water can kill a camera if it gets in the cracks. When I got close enough, I positioned the monopod and waited for a flight sequence. This bird is a true straight arrow in flight. The Bahamas National Trust was very gracious to allow me access to this protected sanctuary for its beloved national symbol.

Page87 Red-billed Tropicbird
Isabel Island, Mexico (December 2000) *Nikon F5, 600mm f4 lens, Fuji Provia 100*

The moment that I laid eyes on this graceful flier, I fell in love. A few dozen tropicbirds nest on Isabel Island amidst a thriving booby and frigatebird colony. One cliff in particular was favored as it featured lots of rocky crevices where a nest could be concealed. For three afternoons in a row, I stood vigil on the cliff waiting for the birds to return from a day of fishing out to sea. They were in no particular hurry to land by the nest, instead wheeling in giant loops over the cove. I was able to see the beautiful markings on the bird's topside because of my high perch. They show lovely details difficult to see from a boat. The long, fanciful tail seems a fitting adornment for a bird nesting on such a lush tropical island.

Page88 Tundra Swans
Magothy River, Maryland (January 2000) *Nikon F5, 600mm f4 lens, Fuji Provia 100*

Magic happens with regularity at Byran's pier along the Chesapeake Bay when scoops of corn are tossed out. Waterfowl within a mile radius know the que and gather for the feast. For several years, the same group of Tundra Swans has wintered on this particular creek due to the generosity of two families at opposite ends that feed the waterfowl daily. The corn really helps to offset the Bay's decline of submerged aquatic vegetation. The graceful swans fly over in small groups and make passes before landing. When shooting groups, I will stop down my aperture to f8 or f11 for additional depth-of-field to make as many birds as possible in focus. I also push my film one stop for extra speed.

Page88, 89 Mute Swan
Tred Avon River, Maryland (June 1999) *Nikon F5, 300mm f2.8 lens, Kodak E100 VS*

Waking up to calm waters on the bay, I was inspired to attempt shots of Mute Swans from my kayak. It didn't take long to find a pair that had been nesting on this creek for several years. As I approached, the birds were getting antsy, being confined to a small cove. My drifting kayak blocked the escape route and I sensed that the action would pick up momentarily. I was ready when the bird took flight. The 300mm f2.8 lens on an F5 is a heavy load, so I opened up the aperture to maximize shutter speed. The male splashed across the still water to generate sufficient momentum for liftoff. The background photographed black when I exposed for the bright plumage.

Page90 Trumpeter Swans
Hennepin Park, Minnesota (September 1999) *Nikon F5, 600mm f4 lens with 1.4x TC, Fuji Velvia 50*

This moment ranks as one of the top ten highlights of the entire project. A good deal of planning went into putting myself in a position to photograph wild Trumpeter Swans. I had a blissful morning shoot with this family of six on a misty autumn day. The remote lake was large and the birds could have kept a distance so that no photographs were taken. However, they favored the sunny side of the lake and I shot to my heart's content. At one point, a fledgling took off to circle the lake. One of the adults also took off to escort junior on his training mission. After hugging the far shore, the tandem flew right at me and banked at just the right moment to fill the frame.

Page92 Osprey
Tred Avon River, Maryland (July 2002) *Nikon F5, 600mm f4 lens, Fuji Provia 400*

This was my first test shoot with the new Provia 400 film. I was pleasantly surprised at how tight the grain was though the colors were not quite as punchy. A close friend of the family told me of an Osprey that he had conditioned to swoop down and snatch expired fish that he threw out from his dock. I had to see this for myself. Sure enough, he threw one out and the large raptor attacked the target with precision. However, I missed the shot of talons plunging into the water, as she was too fast and close to the dock. On the next round, I waited for her to approach the nest with the clutched fish, allowing plenty of time for autofocus to lock on. Nearly a dozen frames in the sequence were tack sharp, a real bonus.

Page93 Snail Kite
Lake Kissimmee, Florida (April 1999) *Nikon F5, 600mm f4 lens, Fuji Sensia 100*

On the advice of an associate, I hired an airboat captain for three days of shooting on Lake Kissimmee in Central Florida. This pristine wetland boasts a healthy colony of Snail Kites, which nest in reeds just a few feet above the water. We were unable to pinpoint any shootable nests, but over a dozen kites were seen flying about while hunting apple snails, its main food source. We watched this female Snail Kite pluck a snail from the shallows and fly overhead with her prize. I had no idea she would land close to the boat to feed. The wings are spread eagle for an instant so brief that you cannot expect such a shot. Even at eight frames per second, a bird's wings take on many contortions during a one-second interval.

Page93 Swallow-tailed Kite
Anhinga Trail, Florida (March 1999) *Nikon F5, 600mm f4 lens with 1.4x TC, Fuji Velvia 50*

This is a special delivery bird sent by the angels... it came seemingly from out of nowhere, made one low pass in front of a spellbound audience and promptly disappeared into the marsh. I was heading back to the parking lot after a great morning shoot when I heard some birders making a fuss. Since I shoot on a monopod, I was able to set up in a few seconds and scan for the special bird. I only got off three frames before the ghost passed over the trail and was gone. This was my first and only shoot to date with this raptor. A fellow in a wheelchair also took some pictures and was elated, an answer to a prayer he later recounted. He spoke with the glee of a kid in a candy store.

Photography Notes

Page 94 Bald Eagle
Homer, Alaska
(January 1999)
Nikon F5, 600mm f4 lens, Fuji Provia 100

While shooting from Jean's yard, I noticed a pair of parallel poles where eagles frequently perched during the daily feeding frenzy. Once a salmon fillet is scored, an eagle typically flies far away to eat in peace or lands on one of the set-up perches to feast. The birds far outnumber the perches as they constantly jockey for position and squabble over squatting rights. This shot was planned out well in advance. I pre-focused on the two perches and left additional space on top to accommodate the approach of additional birds. Fortunately, two birds were on the same focal plane as they eyed the left-hand pole. The darker juvenile bird beat him to it by less than a second, as the salmon fillet was ferried off to another perch.

Page 97 Mallard, Canvasback
Magothy River, Maryland
(February 2000) *Nikon F5, 600mm f4 lens with 1.4x TC, Fuji Provia 100*

These photographs of classic Chesapeake waterfowl were made on different days, but the game plan was the same: throw out some corn at the end of the pier on a clear winter afternoon and sit low, camera anchored to a Whimberly head as the ducks, swans and geese flew into the area. My shoot would typically start three hours before sunset. Single flying ducks are one of the most challenging subjects in nature photography. These speeding bullets need to be very close with a huge lens, something most wild ducks avoid like the plague. It takes lots of practice to train hand-eye coordination for flight photography. Autofocus does get confused and missed opportunities are common.

Page 101 Black-footed Albatross
Off Newport, Oregon
(May 2001) *Nikon F5, 80-400mm 4.5 zoom lens, Kodak E100 VS*

I had to see that elusive, awe-inspiring nomad of the open ocean—the albatross. I booked two one-day trips with Greg Gullison, a leader of pelagic trips. This shoot is blind faith, searching for a needle in a big haystack. Even if you see an albatross, getting a publishable photo is a tall order as they need to be very close with blue water. Large telephoto lenses are useless on a boat rocking on ocean swells 50 miles offshore. Nearly a dozen Black-footed Albatross were attracted to the chum line offered in exchange for a close fly-by. These birds are fighting over scraps. Rarely do I get seasick, but this day was one horrific exception. It took an ocean of willpower to attempt photographs while heaving my guts out.

Page 104 Purple Sandpiper
Ocean City, Maryland
(April 1994) *Nikon F3, 600mm f4 lens, Fuji Sensia 100*

This shot was made during my first years of wildlife photography while working on *Maryland's Great Outdoors*. Spring is a great time to see a variety of migrating waterbirds at the main jetty in Ocean City. This nutrient-rich channel connects the Atlantic with coastal bays sheltered by barrier islands. At low tide, seaweed-covered boulders make for picturesque perches for various shorebirds. This subject was approached very slowly as shorebirds are easily spooked. I watched for signs of agitation, but this fellow seemed quite comfortable with me. I got down low to frame the bird with a water backdrop. A monopod is really handy when working on slippery rocks with skittish birds.

Page 96 Bufflehead
Magothy River, Maryland
(February 2000) *Nikon F5, 600mm f4 lens with 1.4x TC, Fuji Provia 100*

When corn is thrown out at a friend's pier on the Chesapeake Bay, all sorts of waterfowl gather for the feast. Of the half dozen species that were regulars, the Bufflehead were always the most wary, often feeding only after the other birds had gotten their fill and moved on. I loved watching their splayed pink webs deployed for a water-ski landing. One afternoon, seeing about twenty white dots across the creek, I was determined to try for the shot and pass up on other birds. At first the Bufflehead would land far away, but they kept coming closer. Finally a few birds flew at me and landed when filling nearly half the frame, maybe forty feet away. This was the only day that I got to capture this magic moment.

Page 98 Snow Geese & Mallards
Bosque del Apache NWR, New Mexico
(November 1998) *Nikon F5, 600mm f4 lens with 1.4x TC, Fuji Provia 100*

My first trip to Bosque was during an Arthur Morris instructional photo tour. We quickly learned how to work the area for maximum opportunity based on his countless missions to this oasis. Our trip coincided with the corn harvest by refuge staff close to the road where we would be viewing the birds. This is key because you are not allowed off-road at Bosque to chase your quarry. Crops are managed for the benefit of waterfowl and cranes who depend on the grains for winter survival. Over the course of the day, there will be many blastoffs when feeding birds are flushed by coyotes. I used autofocus on this shot and got lucky as it can be easily confused when the sensors see the background.

Page 102 Western Gull
Piedras Blancas, California (January 1999) *Nikon F5, 600mm f4.5lens with 1.4x TC, Fuji Provia 100*

A large number of Western Gulls flock to elephant seal birthing areas during the winter months. This huge colony near the Hearst Castle in San Simeon was an unplanned stop for us driving south on Coastal Highway 1. I noticed all of these cars pulled over (in the middle of nowhere) and had to investigate. From the parking lot, it suddenly dawned on me that we were in the midst of hundreds of elephant seals. I did not see any births that afternoon, so the scavenging gulls were quiet. I noticed this one gull make the rounds as he came upon a day's-old pup nestled against its mother. For one brief moment, the gull looked right into the seal's eyes... what an incredibly sweet moment.

Page 104 Black Turnstone & Spotted Sandpiper
San Diego, California (January 1999) *Nikon F5, 600mm f4 lens with 1.4x TC, Fuji Velvia 50*

After a glorious morning with pelicans at La Jolla, our group ventured to a rocky beach just south of the harbor seal area. An adventurous soul, I decided to scramble over slippery boulders to see if any birds turned up. The terrain was so rough that shooting on a tripod would have been impossible. Both of these birds were photographed feeding on the same stretch of beach. During the hour that I worked this area, the moments of clean poses could be measured in seconds as feeding shorebirds are frenetic. When the head pops up, I take several frames to have a choice for the best angle on the head. Since depth-of-field is limited with 840mm, I manually focus on the bird's eye.

Page 96 Black-bellied Whistling Duck
Corpus Christi, Texas (March 2000) *Nikon F5, 600mm f4 lens with 1.4x TC, Fuji Provia 100*

Our shoot seemed to be over, heading back from the viewing platform at the Hans A. Suter Wildlife Area in Corpus Christi. A variety of shorebirds and ducks rested within camera range and it was a decent shoot. Returning up the trail with my 600mm lens resting on my shoulder, we noticed a group of ducks steaming towards us just over the tree line. I usually try for the lead bird in a group and will shoot the trailers once the leader passes by. This was my first encounter with the Black-bellied Whistling Duck. The bright white patch on the wings certainly helped the autofocus sensors lock on, contrasting starkly with the blue sky. Tight shots of flying ducks are hard to come by.

Page 100 Black-crowned Night-Heron
Druid Hill Park, Maryland (May 1999) *Nikon N90s, 600mm f4 lens, Fuji Sensia 100*

There is a wonderful farm pond exhibit at The Baltimore Zoo with a few floating logs that attract basking turtles and water snakes. The stocked pond also attracts wild Black-crowned Night-Herons that nest in the vicinity. During this visit to the zoo, one heron was giving champion poses on a sculpted branch overlooking the water. Out of the blue, he stabbed at a goldfish and swallowed it within seconds. It was so sudden that I didn't get any shots. I decided to wait and see if he would fish again. Within the hour, he took the plunge and this time it was a bigger fish that required grappling to subdue. There was no depth-of-field here, so I focused on the fish.

Page 103 Herring Gull
Stone Harbor, New Jersey (October 1998) *Nikon N90s, 600mm f4 lens with 1.4x TC, Fuji Velvia 50*

Artie brought his group to shoot flying terns and roosting shorebirds at this lovely spot north of Cape May. He mentioned seeing gulls eating crabs during prior visits and I made up my mind that I would try for such a shot. The plan was to hang with gulls fishing in the surf and see what showed up. Plucked from the saltwater, this poor crab is putting on his best defense, but it was a hopeless case to plead in front of a hungry judge. Despite the disarming of the crab that followed, I sensed a moment of respect for the crab as his captor knows that such treats from the ocean are his sustenance. I felt bad for the crab, but I know that it is all part of God's plan, just as our tribe enjoys succulent Chesapeake blue crabs.

Page 105 Ruddy Turnstone
Ocean City, Maryland (March 2000) *Nikon F5, 600mm f4 lens, Kodak E100 VS*

Maryland Public Television asked me to shoot some of my favorite wildlife venues for a show they were producing on local photographers. I suggested the Ocean City Inlet, which had been productive on many other occasions. I was a little concerned about making art on demand, not to mention having a camera pointed at me while recording my stream-of-consciousness. We found a small group of turnstones, but since the angle to the sun was tough, I felt challenged. I hung with it and noticed a band of sparkling highlights in the surf. By carefully choosing my angle, I was able to line up one Ruddy Turnstone against the orange glitter. The bird turned his head just far enough to catch sidelight, a critical detail.

Rhapsody In Blue

Page 106 Short-billed Dowitchers
Port Mahon, Delaware (May 1998) *Nikon F5, 600mm f4 lens, Fuji Provia 100*

I made this habitat portrait on my first visit to Port Mahon, where an unpaved road runs parallel to the Delaware Bay shoreline. I heard about this spot in a magazine article and timed my visit to peak shorebird migration in May. Here, thousands of northbound Red Knots, Ruddy Turnstones, Sanderlings and a host of others flock to feast on tiny horseshoe crab eggs deposited in the sand. This rich protein will fuel flight muscles pumping towards Arctic breeding grounds. My visit coincided with low-tide and the beach was covered with horseshoe crabs. Using my car as a blind, I captured this group of dowitchers shortly before sunset. I was really excited to see the birds perched on the crabs.

Page 109 Brown Pelican & Laughing Gull
Sarasota Bay, Florida (December 2000) Nikon F5, 600mm f4 lens, Kodak E100 VS

This juvenile pelican had worked very hard for this scrap of fish guts tossed out at a nearby dock, beating a dozen other pelicans for the prize. He flew off to eat in private. The ever-observant Laughing Gull was watching the whole drama and moved in for the heist. He perched on the pelican's head for the perfect point of attack; the pelican must lift its bill up high to swallow the fish, the exact moment of vulnerability. The gull scooped up the meal and flew off with the bonanza much to the pelican's dismay. One year earlier I watched gulls hunting from the tops of pelicans' heads, but didn't see a heist. Any dock in Florida where fish are regularly cleaned can provide these wonderful opportunities.

Page 112 Least Bittern
Lake Kissimmee, Florida (April 1999) *Nikon F5 600mm f4 lens, Kodak E100 VS*

I was very surprised by how close we were getting to birds at Lake Kissimmee with our noisy airboat. It's a huge lake with very little boat traffic and I'm sure that these birds do not see many people. We were heading back to the dock after a successful day of photographing Snail Kites when I spotted this bittern at the edge of the marsh. Captain Ben didn't see me signal to slow down right away and we almost ran this bird over. I fully expected this notoriously shy bird to disappear into the tangle upon our intrusion, but she was determined to a have a few more minnows. We sat with her for nearly an hour as the light grew prettier right before sunset. We were practically on top of the bird as she fished.

Page 114 Great Blue Heron
Anhinga Trail, Florida (March 1999) *Nikon F5 600mm f4 lens with 1.4x TC, Fuji Sensia 100*

On our second big trip to Florida, Bob Rinker and I brought a pair of walkie-talkies to maximize each other's chance of getting in on a good shoot. Bob watched this heron take a monster fish and called me immediately. I hesitated at first because it was at the far end of the trail and heron's swallow their prey as quickly as possible. My Type A personality kicked in as I scrambled down the canal where a crowd had gathered on a deck to take in the spectacle. I was relieved to see that the heron was still struggling to finish off his catch. I maneuvered into a good position as the crowd sensed my intentions and kindly accommodated me. Monopods are ideal for tight situations like this one.

Page 108 Magnificent Frigate-bird & Blue-footed Booby
Isabel Island, Mexico (December 2000) *Nikon F5, 300mm f4 lens, Fuji Velvia 50*

On our voyage to Isabel Island, we stopped at a goliath rock jutting out of the ocean to observe perched seabirds. Our guide, Armando, told of how frigate-birds will attack boobies and other seabirds in an attempt to pirate fish. It sounded fascinating, but I didn't expect to see it for myself. The seas were choppy, so I was using a hand-held flight lens in case anything came our way. From out of nowhere, a frigatebird spirals up to intercept a Blue-footed Booby. I whipped the camera into position and fired, operating on pure instinct as there was no time to think about the shot. I doubted that autofocus was able to kick-in as I jerked the camera to frame the erratic flight of the duo.

Page 110 Bald Eagles
Homer, Alaska (March 2003) *Nikon F5, 300mm f4 lens, Kodak E100 VS*

Since the eagles on Homer Spit are used to being fed in the winter, a few in our group decided to toss out frozen sardines from the local bait shop to see what happened. There was no feeding frenzy like the breakfast scene at the Eagle Lady's place, but a handful of birds would always be around and venture in for the offering. Over the course of four days, we must have thrown out 300 fish. You cannot appreciate how agile and fast these giant birds are until you see one swoop down in front of you. It was very challenging to keep them in the frame. Out of approximately 100 attack sequences photographed, maybe a dozen frames stood out. Thank God for all the sun we had on this trip since flight photography on overcast days is very disappointing.

Page 113 Green Heron
Wakodahatchee Wetlands, Florida (March 1999) *Nikon F5 600mm f4 lens, Fuji Provia 100*

Life is good for nature photographers at Wakodahatchee Wetlands Preserve near Boynton Beach on Florida's Atlantic Coast. Since the boardwalk makes many turns in the marsh, there are plenty of opportunities in morning and afternoon light. Abundant emergent vegetation creates a lush setting for various waterbirds. The reclusive Green Heron is common here and it's possible to spot several during one loop of the boardwalk if you are a patient observer. Clinging to reeds, this one is extending his long neck to prepare for a strike. A moment later, he was so stretched out I couldn't fit the bird in the frame without backing up. This image was made late in the day when the light is more flattering.

Page 115 Great Black-backed Gull
Cape May, New Jersey October 2001 *Nikon N90s, 600mm f4 lens with 1.4x TC, Fuji Provia 100*

After a nice morning session at Cape May Meadows, I had an inkling to drive down the road to Sunset Beach, where you'll never know what you're going to find. Not far from the parking lot, Kristie spotted a huge gull fumbling with a shark. He eventually flew off disappointed, so we walked over to investigate. This marooned shark was well over a foot long and I wasn't surprised that the gull was unsuccessful. As we backed off the gull circled around. Sure enough, he resumed manipulating the great fish, so I rushed back to the car for the big lens and hoofed it back to the beach. For the next half-hour, he struggled to get a good grip and was finally able to swallow it whole.

Page 109 White Ibis & Snowy Egret
Estero Lagoon, Florida (February 2001) Nikon F5, 600mm f4 lens, Fuji Provia 100

Despite taking hundreds of photos of White Ibis and Snowy Egrets at Estero and elsewhere in Florida, I am always game to see if I can make something new. On this evening, I saw a behavior unknown to me. Several egrets were stalking the ibis, hoping to strike at whatever the ibis startled up. Since the ibis feeds by probing the soft bottom with its lengthy bill, it didn't seem to mind a straggler nabbing the leftovers. I took several rolls as the egret held tight on the ibis's trail. The Snowy Egret appears rather small when sneaking behind the ibis. The shots were taken while wading into the lagoon. This area is not a park, so it is acceptable to walk into the water provided you are respectful of birds.

Page 112 Bald Eagles
Homer, Alaska (January 1999) *Nikon N90s, 28-200 f4.5 zoom lens, Fuji Sensia 100*

Such a shot would not be possible without the Eagle Lady of Homer, who has fed eagles for many years on Homer Spit. Several upturned trees have been strategically "planted" to serve as prime perches for feeding eagles. I stationed myself under the main tree in the corner of her yard and waited for her birds to land with salmon fillets. The light was dreary for much of this first trip to Homer, so I popped on a TTL flash with a slight underexposure. Had I not used the flash, the image would have been flat and uninspiring. Over 100 eagles were stationed in Homer during my shoot. It was a dream come true to watch them do their thing at close range. In Maryland, I'm used to seeing them as a speck on the horizon.

Page 113 Green Heron
Anhinga Trail, Florida (March 2001) *Nikon F5 600mm f4 lens with 1.4x TC, Kodak E100 VS*

I cannot think of a better spot to photograph Green Herons than along the main canal at the Anhinga Trail in Everglades National Park. Fish are concentrated here in great numbers, as are the birds who hunt them (as well as photographers). Lots of branches and reeds line the shallow canal, making for ideal Green Heron habitat. So many people visit here daily that a great variety of species are pretty used to the stares, finger-pointing and long tele-photo lenses. Here the long neck is tucked in until a target is spotted. I carefully selected the background to be a dark patch of water reflecting a shaded area. Just moving a few steps to the side can make a dramatic difference in a photograph's effectiveness.

Page 115 Reddish Egret
Estero Lagoon, Florida (March 1998) *Nikon F5 600mm f4 lens, Fuji Velvia 50*

I heard that Estero was a good spot to see the white phase Reddish Egret, so we checked it out. Lots of birds were shootable, but no Reddish Egret. On our way back, I saw what looked like a Great Egret flying towards us. When it landed fifty feet away, I knew then that my Reddish had just appeared. It was awesome to focus my lens and see those beautiful pink lores on its face. He must have caught four or five minnows in twenty minutes. This one jumped out as it had stripes on its side. Because it was a larger minnow, it took the bird a while to position the fish properly for headfirst swallowing. On future trips to the area, I stayed at Ft. Myers Beach such that this magical lagoon was just footsteps away.

Photography Notes

Page 116 Great Blue Heron
Oscar Shearer Park, Florida (March 1998) *Nikon F5 600mm f4 lens, Fuji Provia 100*

This is the shot that set this project in motion, five years traveling the continent's limits searching for beautiful waterbirds. When Rinker and I approached this heron grappling with a muskrat, I didn't think that he would stick around for a photo session. This was a bittersweet moment as the muskrat was still alive, and I have developed empathy for any type of animal in distress. I realized that the heron worked hard for this meal and it would provide good nourishment. I managed to shoot one roll before the heron flew off with its mammal, still gripped by the bill. It would be ten days before the film was processed and these were very long days indeed as I was dying to see how the images turned out.

Page 119 Herring Gulls
Deal Island, Maryland (June 1994) *Nikon F3, 600mm f4 lens with 1.4x TC, Fujichrome 100*

This image never made the final cut for the *Maryland's Great Outdoors* book, but it has found a home here. While traveling to a Black-necked Stilt nesting area on the Chesapeake Bay, these gulls caught my attention as they played tug-of-war. At first glance, I thought they were on their nest, but I then realized that it was a feeding platform. When both heads were raised, I could discern bone, but wasn't sure if it was a bird or mammal carcass they were picking at. Sometimes wonderful photo ops take you by surprise; you just have to be observant and flexible with your schedule. If the potential for a nice picture is developing, don't rush off to the next thing.

Page 121 Anhinga
Anhinga Trail, Florida (February 2001) *Nikon F5, 600mm f4 lens with 1.4x TC, Fuji Velvia 50*

After watching this male Anhinga catch a variety of fish in the main channel, I fondly named him the "Bassmaster." I was determined to get a shot of him with a big fish, so I concentrated on him the last day of our visit here. My patience was really being tested. After watching one unsuccessful dive after another, I was tempted to work herons just down the path. However, I didn't want to miss the big one. After an hour or two, he finally popped up with a nice bass speared on the bill. He then hauled out on a rock to finish the job. I moved several feet to my left to put the bird against blue water background instead of brown reeds. Seconds later, the fish was traveling down the snakebird's neck.

Page 123 Lesser Scaup
Bolsa Chica, California (January 2001) *Nikon F5, 600mm f4 lens with 2x TC, Fuji Provia 100*

There must be a huge concentration of seafood by the floodgates that open to Bolsa Chica's main lagoon. During each of my winter visits in 1999, 2001 and 2003, I have always seen a host of ducks and other waterbirds at this spot. Scaup have a fondness for mussels, which they can crack open with their stout blue bills. This was the largest mussel gathered that morning that I could see. The duck positioned it perfectly in its mouth to show off the shell's contour. This shot was made several hours after sunrise, certainly not the most flattering light, but it is still a worthwhile image. Don't be averse to shooting when it is bright as plenty of opportunities can pass you by if you're too rigid.

Page 118 Glaucous Gull
Pribilof Islands, Alaska (July 1998) *Nikon N90s, 600mm f4 lens with 2x TC, Fuji Provia 100*

I didn't expect to photograph gulls at the northern fur seal rookery on St. Paul Island. I was unaware of their fondness of afterbirth, a highly coveted nutrition windfall. We were only allowed to photograph the colony from a blind. This image was made on a monopod with 1200mm, a dicey shoot on overcast days as I could only manage a shutter speed of 1/125 with the film pushed one stop. I selected this frame as the "meat" stands out against the dark background. The newborn pup is not visible from this angle, but an adult female balances out the left hand of the image to help tell the story. I didn't realize that this was an immature Glaucous Gull until researching the captions years later.

Page 119 Hybrid Gull
Monterey, California (January 1999) *Nikon F5, 600mm f4 lens, Fuji Provia 100*

I was desperately in search of the Black Oystercatcher and heard that Sunset Drive was a premier area to look. Lots of people were strolling the beach on this heavenly Sunday afternoon, which makes for acclimated birds. I walked past a group of gulls, intent on finding the oystercatcher, when my head suddenly turned in the direction of one peculiar bird holding a starfish. At this point, it was a truce; the gull was no longer fumbling with its prey to attempt swallowing. The angle to the sun was not ideal, but I was able to work several different compositions to take advantage of this amazing opportunity. A colleague from Cape May later identified this bird as a likely hybrid of a Western Gull and a Glaucous-winged Gull.

Page 122 Wood Ducks
Patterson Park, Maryland (August 2001) *Nikon F5, 600mm f4 lens, Kodak E100 VS*

This is one of nearly 20 perches that I set at the boat lake in Baltimore City's Patterson Park during my four-year project documenting the resident Wood Ducks. On most mornings there was at least one woodie on this perch resting or preening. On rare occasions, these dabbling ducks would eat duckweed from the perch. This is the only time that I saw two summer drakes eating simultaneously. The post-molt summer plumage of the Wood Duck renders it a very different looking bird, yet still dramatic with huge red eyes and bill. When you return to a favorite spot time and again, a great variety of wonderful moments show up. I guess I visited this lake at least 200 times between 1999 and 2004.

Page 124 Canvasbacks & Mallards
Magothy River, Maryland (February 2000) *Nikon F5, 300mm f2.8 lens, Kodak E100 VS*

I received a phone call from a lovely Severna Park woman who asked me to speak to her photography club. While chatting about waterfowl, I received an invitation to photograph the Tundra Swans that she and her husband feed each winter on the Chesapeake Bay. A variety of ducks also converge at their dock when corn is thrown out. For this shoot, ice had formed on the bay and really concentrated the birds in a small pool of water. I threw out plenty of corn, so all could partake in the feast, including two Canada Geese. This photo implies plentiful waterfowl, but many duck species, including the Canvasback, are greatly reduced from historic levels due to declining aquatic vegetation across the bay.

Page 118 Herring Gull
Cape May, New Jersey (October 2000) *Nikon F5, 600mm f4 lens with 1.4x TC, Fuji Provia 100*

Two years prior, I photographed gulls catching crabs at Stone Harbor and history was about to repeat itself. I had never seen a gull hunt crabs in Maryland. Perhaps there were different crabs here on the Jersey Shore that fit the bill. This type of shoot tests your skills since it happens so quickly. The gull will dispatch and ingest crabs as soon as possible, before another bird tries to take it away. Thrashing movements are used to break off the claws and some frames will be soft due to the fast action. I'm always looking for that brief window when the bird pauses long enough to guarantee a sharp picture. I was fortunate that the crab was displayed so clearly in this frame, brandishing its claws in vehement protest.

Page 120 Double-crested Cormorants
Anhinga Trail, Florida (February 2001) *Nikon F5, 600mm f4 lens with 1.4x TC, Fuji Provia 100*

One of the most entertaining "shows" I've ever seen is the cormorant feeding frenzy at the main pond at Royal Palm. For the better part of the day, several dozen cormorants feasted on big fish concentrated in the alligator pool. It seemed like every five minutes, another bird would pop up with a nice fish in its bill, thrashing to break free from its captor. Anhingas also work this fishing hole, but in smaller numbers. As soon as the bird pops up, it attempts to swallow the fish before it slips away or another cormorant pirates the meal. This is a great setting for shooting on a monopod as there are mere seconds to find your subject, focus, compose and shoot.

Page 123 Brandt
Jamaica Bay, New York (April 2000) *Nikon F5, 600mm f4 lens with 1.4x TC, Fuji Provia 100*

I asked Artie to recommend a good spot for Brandt and he kindly suggested Jamaica Bay in April, when birds frequent a popular beach. At other times, this small goose tends to keep a distance, excluding opportunities for portraits. I made the trip that spring and there were dozens of Brandt milling about close to shore. I even saw a few birds standing on the beach, nearly as tame as gulls. Over two days, I shot nearly thirty rolls of the Brandt. I like how this image implies a sense of community; one bird is usually on the lookout for danger while others are tipped-up grazing on submerged vegetation in the shallows. A moment later, they swapped roles.

Page 126 American White Pelican
Sarasota Bay, Florida (December 2000) *Nikon F5, 600 mm f4 lens, Fuji Provia 100*

My friend, Artie, told me how he bought some sardines at a bait shop in Florida and tossed them out at a dock where American White Pelicans were known to congregate. Meandering around Sarasota Bay with no particular plan, I passed a bait shop and the memory popped up. I pulled over and bought a bucket of large sardines, not knowing where I would use them. Boat ramps are a great place to photograph birds, especially when fishermen return to clean their catch. I passed one such place and pulled over on a hunch. When I threw out the sardines, pelicans started to come in from across the bay to join the gulls already there. Within minutes, I had a dozen giant pelicans vying for handouts.

Rhapsody In Blue

Page 127 Brown Pelican
Sarasota Bay, Florida
(January 2000) *Nikon
F5, 600mm f4 lens
with 1.4x TC,
Kodak E100 VS*

Local fishermen usually toss out undesirable fish scraps when cleaning their catch dockside. The pelicans are no dummies... why work harder than you have to for a meal. Towards the afternoon when charter boats return, several dozen pelicans congregate at this spot that I discovered by chance. Dramatic tug-of-war battles are not uncommon as this trio demonstrates. Gulls will get into the act and claim their fair share. The action was so heated that I blazed through an entire roll of 36 frames in less than a minute, almost like shooting a video clip from which I could select peak moments. With multiple birds, I usually stop down my aperture to f8 or f11 (light permitting) to have more of the group in focus.

Page 129 Limpkin
Loxahatchee NWR, Florida
(March 1999) *Nikon F5,
600mm f4 lens, Fuji Velvia 50*

One year prior, I photographed a Limpkin at Loxahatchee, but was not able to make a strong image as the bird held tight in a cluster of reeds. Returning a year later, I thought we would find another easily, but we searched for most of the morning to no avail. A pair of Loggerhead Shrikes caught our attention, though, and we worked them for an hour at close range. Such is birding in Florida... never a dull moment. On the walk back to the car, Bob spotted a Limpkin by the road with a large apple snail. I only got off three frames before the bird disappeared into the marsh, not to be seen again. Since this is a secretive, elusive species, I like all of the vegetation showing how the bird is normally seen.

Page 131 Long-billed Curlew
Newport Bay, California
(January 2001) *Nikon
F5, 600mm f4 lens with
2x TC, Kodak E100 VS*

It pays to have clear intention before starting a wildlife shoot. I am more likely to get the desired results when they are communicated to the powers that be. God hears all requests; when and how they are answered involves some mystery and we learn to surrender control. Before my second big trip to California, I prayed for a feeding curlew at close range. The spot where I thought it might happen, Chula Vista, did not pan out. When I least expected it, the opportunity surfaced several days later. Our group was photographing teal and other dabblers at Newport Back Bay. The receding tide exposed a mud flat and there he was—a single Long-billed Curlew probing the muck for edibles.

Page 132 Snowy Egret
St. Augustine, Florida (March 1999) *Nikon N90s, 600mm f4 lens, Fuji Provia 100*

At this age, chicks are fairly mobile and curious, a dangerous combination when you live above an alligator pond stocked with many large adults. I didn't realize there was a nest in this shrub until an adult Snowy Egret (note the "golden slippers") landed on top and a chick emerged through the foliage to receive a meal. The boardwalk at the alligator farm is a fairly tight space for photographers and using a monopod allows quick set-up without blocking the pathway. The light was somewhat harsh, but the chick angled properly to catch sidelight on the face. Without this element I would have tossed this image. Feeding egret chicks display lots of erratic movement, so I open up for a faster shutter speed.

Page 127 Brown Pelican
Bolsa Chica, California
(January 1999) *Nikon
F5, Tokina 400mm f5.6
lens, Ectochrome 100*

For three glorious days in a row, our workshop group of seven was treated to front row seats of diving Brown Pelicans. On two subsequent visits in 2001 and 2003, no such activity happened by the footbridge at Bolsa Chica. I tried to shoot with my big lens on a monopod, but it was tight for fast-diving subjects, so I switched to my new handheld 400mm Tokina. Fortunately, the autofocus on this affordable lens was good enough to track these diving heavyweights. I guess that I photographed maybe 50 plunge sequences. There is an element of chance to a shot like this as the dives are too quick to intentionally capture the bill about to break the surface of the water. The mouth is opened upon impact.

Page 130 Willet & Marbled Godwit
Santa Barbara, California (January 1999)
Nikon N90s, 600mm f4 lens, Fuji RMS (400)

I was in an unfamiliar area with no scouting report and had a sunny afternoon to kill, so I followed my intuition. Marinas are usually productive spots for birds and I pulled over to investigate a big commercial fishing marina in Santa Barbara. I noticed a small beach at the end of the jetty and I headed for it, where I found a variety of gulls, grebes and shorebirds. This ball of seaweed washed up and a Marbled Godwit began to probe it. The light grew sweeter as I pulled out my last roll of film. Then a Willet joined in and they both jockeyed for position, very willing to share the meal together. For one brief moment, they were on the same focal plain and I had my shot.

Page 131 Lesser Yellowlegs
Cape May, New Jersey
(October 1998) *Nikon
F5, 600mm f4 lens with
1.4x TC, Fuji Provia 100*

One look at the Cape May Meadows that October morning and I was transported to Florida where large concentrations of waterbirds are routine. The water level on the pond was just right for wading birds, dabbling ducks and long-legged shorebirds to harvest the bounty. At first light, a Great Egret caught an eight-inch eel for a memorable shoot. My attention drifted to the yellowlegs; both species were working the shallows by the footpath. I was amazed to see this Lesser Yellowlegs catch an eel. He seemed perplexed as to what to do with it, to the delight of several photographers. On two subsequent visits to the meadows, the water level was higher and there were virtually no birds to photograph.

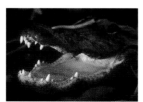

Page 133 American Alligator
Anhinga Trail, Florida
(February 2001) *Nikon
F5, 600mm f4 lens,
Kodak E100 VS*

If you want to photograph wild alligators, I cannot image a better venue than the Anhinga Trail, at Royal Palm in Everglades National Park. They are close and abundant in a lush, beautiful setting. I've heard people say that they have seen gallinules and baby Anhingas being taken by gators. They will also capture wading birds, fish, turtles, snakes and others. This fine specimen was "bellowing" as part of courtship. While hunting he would be fully submerged to launch a surprise attack from below. The sun was on the horizon, just minutes to setting, which made for nice illumination of the mouth. I wonder how many feathers have passed through these pearly gates.

Page 128 Snail Kite
Lake Kissimmee, Florida (April 1999) *Nikon F5, 600mm f4 lens with 1.4x TC, Fuji RMS (200)*

I couldn't have done this project without the help of numerous individuals who tipped me off on great places to see birds. I was rearing to go to Lake Kissimmee when I heard that it hosts a healthy population of nesting Snail Kites. My captain assured me that we would find birds and get close despite the boat's noisy propeller. I had never seen a Snail Kite before, so finding at least a dozen to photograph was like heaven. We came upon this gorgeous male grasping an apple snail with his beak. We drifted by and the bird was remarkably tolerant of our close approach. Many of the birds here are banded, closely monitored by biologists. I was happy to see that this bird was unmarked.

Page 130 American Oystercatcher
Estero Lagoon, Florida
(January 2000) *Nikon
F5, 600mm f4 lens with
1.4x TC, Fuji Provia 100*

When I first started getting into birds during the mid-nineties, I scoured field guides to learn what was out there and soaked it up like a sponge. This species caught my attention and I was delighted to learn that we had them in Maryland. I had always hoped for a dream session with this flamboyant shorebird and it finally happened over a three-day period at Estero Lagoon. I found a pair that was quite tolerant of close approach and I probably shot 20 rolls of them, mostly from a kneeling position. I recommend knee pads for such work. Feeding was fun to shoot since they would extract marine worms from the sandy bottom; vigorous shaking washed them off before consumption.

Page 132 Purple Gallinule
Anhinga Trail, Florida
(March 1999) *Nikon F5,
600mm f4 lens, Fuji
Velvia 50*

Considering the concentration of alligators, it is surprising that any gallinules could survive. However, on each visit to the Royal Palm Visitors' Center in Everglades National Park I've always seen at least one gallinule. A feeding Purple Gallinule is a challenge to photograph, moving erratically across lily pads in thick cover. Ideally, you hope for a bird coming towards you at a slight angle. When I saw this bird flap its lovely wings while hopping around, I knew the shot that I wanted. For this series, I did manual focus since there was little contrast between the subject and background. It was also hard to keep the focus sensors on his body. Two rolls of lily trotting yielded about a half-dozen interesting frames.

Page 133 Coyotes
Bosque del Apache,
New Mexico (November
2000) *Nikon F5,
600mm f4 lens with 2x
TC, Fuji Provia 100*

On my initial visit to Bosque in 1998, I was surprised at how many coyotes we saw though they were always a good distance off, launching attacks on geese and cranes feeding at the farm fields. I never saw a kill since the birds were one step ahead of their pursuers. One morning during our 2000 visit, I turned the corner and saw four coyotes in a field. I popped on the 2x for a close-up view and saw the Snow Goose on the ground. This image is cropped in tight from the original slide as the subjects were maybe 100 yards away. After the coyotes had their fill, a Rough-legged Hawk and a Northern Harrier squabbled over the leftovers... what an unbelievable combination of gorgeous predators.

Photography Notes

Page 134 Roseate Spoonbill
Merritt Island NWR, Florida (April 1999) *Nikon F5, 600mm f4 lens with 1.4x TC, Kodak E100 VS*

Strike while the iron is hot, as the expression goes... I was only scheduled to be at Merritt Island for one day en route to St. Augustine. In late afternoon, spoonbills congregated in the corner of a large impoundment near the road for some great shooting. Since birds are creatures of habit, I figured they might do it the following day, so I stayed an extra night. This shot was made on that second afternoon. It was the best spoonbill shooting of my brief bird photography career. When the preening bird dropped a wing reflecting in blue water, it was a moment of Heaven on Earth. It's always fun to hear non-birders comment, "Look at them beautiful flamingoes, hon!"

Page 135, 136 Glossy Ibis
Jamaica Bay, New York (August 1999) *Nikon N90s, 600mm f4 lens with 2x TC, Kodak E100 VS*

After shooting shorebirds in the muck commando-style, our group of Artie protégés was glad to have a late morning shoot in a comfortable, shaded blind watching wading birds preen and rest. This particular pond is heavily wooded, which makes for gorgeous green water reflecting the summer foliage. The image of a bathing Glossy Ibis was probably taken at 1/125 of a second, slow enough for some motion to register with flying droplets and for the tip of the bill to blur. I refer to this photo as the first documented "spoonbill ibis" due to the exaggerated bill tip. After bathing, the ibis would lift their wings to sunbathe. Getting two in the shot to sunbathe was a miracle.

Page 136, 137 Royal Tern & Red Knot
Estero Lagoon, Florida (January 2000) *Nikon F5, 600mm f4 lens with 1.4x TC, Kodak E100 VS*

I was delighted to discover a handful of Red Knots at Estero in mid-winter, as I thought they all went to South America for the winter. Like virtually all other birds here, the shorebirds can be very tolerant if approached respectfully. It is very important to watch a bird's body language for signs of disturbance. I usually move five or ten paces and stop to provide the subject opportunity to acclimate. With small birds, I try to stay low to the ground for a more intimate vantage point. This Royal Tern was splashing up a storm, allowing me enough time to close the gap slowly without spooking him. Many times I have approached a bird cautiously and it flew off anyway.

Page 137 Redhead
Santee Lakes, California (January 2001) *Nikon F5, 600mm f4 lens with 1.4x TC, Kodak E100 VS*

Santee Lakes is a phenomenal place to photograph upwards of a dozen duck species. Mixed in with some Ruddy, Wood and Ring-necked Ducks was a lone Redhead seen three days in a row on that particular trip. It accepted handouts and was lured close to shore. After having its fill, it started to bathe at close range, a sign that the bird was very comfortable in our presence. This was not a prolonged bath, but a mini-bath that provided just enough splashing for a few good shots. At least once a day, most birds do a serious cleaning with lots of dunking and splashing. To capture water beading on the plumage, I shot lots of frames on high motor drive to increase the chances of a standout frame.

Page 138 Great Blue Heron
Merritt Island NWR, Florida (April 1999) *Nikon F5, 600mm f4 lens, Kodak E100 VS*

This was my first experience with a wading bird sunbath. The wings are dropped spread-eagle to gather bright sunlight which tends to make feather parasites scatter when, alas, they are more easily removed by preening. During the five years of shooting for this book, I have only seen this posture three other times with Great Blue Herons and once with a Yellow-crowned Night Heron. I stumbled upon this bizarre pose which was held long enough to shoot one or two rolls and made a conscious effort to work every angle possible of a fleeting opportunity. A few minutes later, the wings were tucked in and the shoot was over.

Page 138 Double-crested Cormorants
Sanibel Island, Florida (February 1993) *Nikon F3, 600mm f4 lens, Fuji Velvia 50*

This image was made five years before working on *Rhapsody in Blue*... a sign of things to come. I fondly remember family vacations as a teenager, especially the Sanibel trip. Our visit to Ding Darling NWR in the late 1970's gave me a front row seat to a waterbird extravaganza the likes of which I had only seen on *Wild Kingdom*. Sanibel was an easy choice in 1993 for a romantic getaway with a girlfriend. I couldn't wait to focus my new 600mm lens on all those birds. Each day, we looped several times as things are always changing. This prime perch featured roosting cormorants on our last pass of the day. What makes the shot work is sidelight catching the left-most cormorant's face.

Page 139 Anhinga
Corkscrew Swamp, Florida (February 2001) *Nikon F5, 600mm f4 lens, Kodak E100 VS*

During my ten trips to Florida for this project, I have photographed dozens of posturing Anhingas, but never had all of the elements click until this scene at Corkscrew Swamp, operated by the National Audubon Society. I believe that this pond along the boardwalk is called Lettuce Lake, covered from one end to the other with vibrant green plants. We watched this Anhinga hunt the small pond ringed by ancient bald cypress trees. After catching a few small fish, he popped up on this perfect basking log to dry off his soaked plumage. The bird was always moving his head around, as he wouldn't want an alligator to sneak up and grab him. I waited until the bill turned fully for a nice profile.

Page 140 Sandhill Cranes
Bosque del Apache, New Mexico (November 1998) *Nikon N90s, 600mm f4 lens, Fuji Provia 100*

For our last shoot of the day, we were working the pond near the main entrance where geese congregate close to the road at sunset. I noticed a group of cranes far to the right and decided to work them since getting close-ups of cranes can be difficult at Bosque. Upon choosing my spot, one of the birds started to vocalize dramatically. Another reciprocated and they all got into it. When one bird suddenly leaped, I fired away. Fortunately, both quarreling birds were on the same focal plain as there was little depth-of-field. I love how the head of the leaper is framed by blue water; if it was just inches lower, the picture would not work as well.

Page 141 Tundra Swans
Magothy River, Maryland (February 2001) *Nikon F5, 600mm f4 lens with 1.4x TC, Fuji Provia 100*

Tundra Swans are among the most quarrelsome birds I have come across in my years as an avid birder. I photographed them at this creek on the Chesapeake Bay over a dozen times, and have always seen tempers flare among the birds concentrated at feeding time. Though joyous to behold so many swans, I've had trouble getting clean shots with uncluttered backgrounds. On this occasion, I saw a small group off to the side of the main flock. I didn't have to wait long before tensions boiled over and they were neck-biting. I love how the bird on the left balances out the composition, as well as his attempt to clear the scene while the other two duke it out.

Page 142 Western Gulls
Monterey, California (January 1999) *Nikon N90s, 28-200mm f4.5 zoom lens, Fuji Provia 100*

While absorbing the breathtaking scenery of Monterey's famed 17-Mile Drive, I noticed a group of large gulls roosting on a cliff. As I approached, more gulls were flying in for potential handouts from the tourists. The heavy skies and crashing waves created a lot of mood, so I opted for habitat shots instead of close-ups. I popped on my Nikon Speedlight for fill-flash to brighten up the birds. The key to the shot was anticipation. I had the composition set with my finger on the trigger, waiting for birds to appear. Fortunately, I tripped the shutter at the peak moment of wing extension. Never underestimate the "sunshine" in your camera bag, as fill-flash can create magic in otherwise somber lighting.

Page 144 Common Loon
Lake Alamoosook, Maine (July 2001) *Nikon F5, 600mm f4 lens with 1.4x TC, Fuji Velvia 50*

I couldn't have done this shot without the dedicated paddling of my wife, Kristie, as we tried to position the canoe for the best angle. For two days, we worked a family of loons that nested on this huge lake by our lodge. At times, we were very close to the adults and single chick and everyone seemed relaxed. Other times, the birds were more guarded and maintained a bigger safety zone. This adult had been swimming by himself when he suddenly reared up and made quite a ruckus, dancing across the water. It all happened so quickly that I really depended on reflexes and autofocus, which can kick in as fast as lightning. A moment later, the bird dove and we did not see him resurface.

Page 145 American Oystercatcher
Estero Lagoon, Florida (January 2000) *Nikon F5, 600mm f4 lens, Fuji Velvia 50*

This is one of my favorite shots from my dream shoot with a very tolerant pair of American Oystercatchers that I photographed on three consecutive days. I figured that since I had a pair that would allow a very close approach, I might as well try to record as many behaviors as possible. The double-wing stretch was on my wish list, but it is a fleeting moment that requires a lot of patience. A bird can be roosting for hours and then suddenly it is alarmed or intends to move on and needs a good stretch after a nap. The stretch may last only two seconds; you have to be at the ready. I took off the teleconverter ahead of time to allow room for the outstretched wings.

Rhapsody In Blue

Page 145 Reddish Egret
Estero Lagoon, Florida (December 2000) *Nikon F5, 600mm f4 lens with 1.4x TC, Kodak E100 VS*

Many of the wading birds at Estero are very workable and this beauty was no exception. Initially it was perched on a post and I made some preening shots. Since there were no other birds in the vicinity, I decided to hang with the Reddish Egret and see what happened. Shortly thereafter, the bird flew to the water and proceeded to feed in typical helter-skelter fashion. Another Reddish Egret flew in and landed maybe fifty feet away. My bird was not happy about it and launched a charge to scare off the intruder. I love how the bird opened its mouth showing bright coloring that you normally don't see. It pays to hang with a good subject and see what (or who) shows up.

Page 146 Mallards
Maryland (January 2000) *Nikon F5, 600mm f4 lens with 1.4x TC, Kodak E100 VS*

Four years and counting, I have been photographing wild Wood Ducks and Mallards in Patterson Park, just a 10 minutes drive from my home in downtown Baltimore. During the first hard freeze, the ducks and coots were reluctant to leave and kept a small portion of the water open by vigilant paddling. I threw out corn to get the birds up on the ice, for a Mallard looks great with its bright orange feet exposed. Mallard drakes can get quarrelsome and these birds were going at it for nearly ten minutes before the challenger flew off. There was only one moment when both birds had each other in a headlock. For action sequences, I take lots of pictures to hopefully capture peak moments like this one.

Page 146 Northern Shoveler
Baltimore Harbor, Maryland (February 2003) *Nikon F5, 600mm f4 lens with 1.4x TC, Kodak E100 VS*

A nice clean portrait of a Northern Shoveler had eluded me for five years while shooting this book. I certainly had seen my fair share of this handsome dabbler, but they tend to be shy and will duck for cover when pursued. Winter 2003 was particularly cold by Maryland standards and ice formed in Baltimore's Inner Harbor. Walking to the gym one afternoon, I took inventory of the local birds by habit. A handful of shovelers immediately caught my attention, especially the ones hauled out on the ice. Bag the gym, I thought, as I raced back to the house to get my gear. Three drakes and two hens gave me great looks that afternoon and the next.

Page 147 Canada Goose
Magothy River, Maryland (February 2000) *Nikon F5, 600mm f4 lens with 1.4x TC, Kodak E100 VS*

Every few years, the Chesapeake Bay partially freezes after several consecutive days of bitter cold. Since waterfowl look great on the ice, I headed to Bryan's pier several times that winter. Many ducks, geese and swans were in view that afternoon, cut off from feeding in the water and eagerly awaiting their daily corn. I selected this bird because he was all alone for an uncluttered view. The soft blue ice really compliments his colors, especially in golden light. The goose had been sleeping, but I waited for him to elongate the neck and turn sideways. It's critical to wait for the head to turn sufficiently to catch the sidelight.

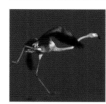

Page 148 Greater Flamingo
Great Inagua, Bahamas (May 2000) *Nikon F5, 600mm f4 lens with 2x TC, Fuji Provia 100*

Autofocus is not supposed to work on the Nikon F5 when a 600mm lens is combined with a 2x teleconverter since the effective aperture is f8. In this situation, I was photographing a preening flamingo while wading out in a saltwater lagoon up to my knees. Something spooked the bird and it took off, running across the water to get airborne. Because it happened so quickly, I clicked on the autofocus and it actually worked at 1200mm. I knew from prior experience that the combination can work in a pinch. I had never seen a flamingo take flight and it was amazing. These wild flamingoes in the Bahamas are generally isolated from people and cannot be approached closely.

Page 148 Sanderling
Stone Harbor, New Jersey (October 2000) *Nikon F5, 600mm f4 lens with 1.4x TC, Fuji Provia 100*

We are all familiar with these high octane sandpipers zooming across the beach where they probe the wettest sand for tiny edibles. For this kind of shot, you have to be right on top of the bird because they are so small. Even at 840mm, this image was cropped in quite a bit. The bird was maybe 25 feet away. I watched the feeding patterns of these Sanderlings in order to position myself correctly. Chasing after the birds doesn't work as they are running away from you, which is not very interesting. I had to anticipate where they would be and wait for them to come to me. My greatest challenge was to keep them centered in the frame while panning rapidly with high magnification. I shot from a kneeling position on a short monopod.

Page 149 American Coot
Patterson Park, Maryland (December 1999) *Nikon F5, 600mm f4 lens with 1.4x TC, Fuji Provia 100*

For several days, I had been working coots on a partially frozen lake in Baltimore. On this day, Christmas morning, I decided to have another go at it as the pond would be completely frozen any day now and the birds would be gone for the rest of the winter. It was a bitter cold morning with only a small section of open water remaining, maybe 60 feet wide. When the coots were not diving for food, they would chase each other around and that's what my heart was set on. I knew that my chances of getting the running shot would never be better with three coots clustered in a small pool. I sat on the ground, camera attached to a Whimberly head on my seldom-used tripod. I shot several running sequences. My plan worked.

Page 150 Harlequin Ducks
Ocean City, Maryland (April 1998) *Nikon N90s, 600mm f4 lens with 2x TC, Fuji Velvia 50*

The key to this shot was patience. The day prior, I spotted about a dozen Harlequins at the Ocean City jetty, but they were skittish and kept a distance—too far for my purposes. I returned the next morning and kept my back to the wall of a motel by the beach to minimize my profile as I moved around. Eventually, the birds hauled out on some boulders, displaying their gorgeous plumage. I must have shot ten rolls that morning as they looked great in the sun. Such opportunities are few-and-far-between, which only makes me appreciate them all the more. I've returned many times to the jetty and never saw even a distant Harlequin. Strike while the iron is hot.

Page 151 Black-bellied Whistling Duck
Corpus Christi, Texas (March 2000) *Nikon F5, 600mm f4 lens with 1.4x TC, Fuji Provia 100*

While scouting for classic Texas songbirds at a remote bird sanctuary outside of Corpus Christi, Bob and I ran into a couple in the parking lot and struck up a conversation. Upon hearing that we were looking for whistling ducks, the lady kindly offered directions to her neighbors' house where wild ducks come in every afternoon for handouts. We showed up at the specified time and there in his yard on the bay were two dozen beautiful ducks with bright red bills—my first ever whistlers. They were leery at the long lenses pointed their way and some flew off, but several stuck around. I chose my angle for an interesting overlap and fired when all the heads were profiled. I never would have found this place if it weren't for the helpful stranger in the parking lot.

Page 152 American White Pelican & Others
Placida, Florida (February 2001) *Nikon F5, 600mm f4 lens with 1.4x TC, Fuji Provia 100*

We hired a pontoon boat out of Placida, south of Ft. Myers, to check out the bird life of Gasparilla Sound. Supposedly, a sandbar drew in lots of pelicans in the afternoon. Sure enough, American White Pelicans descended on the island in small groups two hours before sunset. In sweet light, we had nearly 100 pelicans and a half-dozen other waterbird species. Pontoon boats are great to shoot from because they are very stable even in small waves. I noticed a sole Great Blue Heron had joined the party, so I asked the captain to position the boat to optimize our angle on him. Drifting in the current, I shot when the heron's head was framed between the pelicans.

Page 154 Green Heron
Fort Myers, Florida (February 2001) *Nikon F5, 600mm f4 lens, Fuji Velvia 50*

I usually don't shoot in bright sunlight, but I'm glad that we decided to stop at Three Lakes County Park after a great morning shoot at Estero. There is a boardwalk at this little known spot outside Ft. Myers. Towards lunchtime, we were wrapping up a nice visit when I saw this Green Heron hop up on a branch. He started to preen, so I got into position. A full-wing extension was a bonus as you don't always see that with a preening bird. I love the shot as it is the only time I've seen a Green Heron do such a maneuver, though it is undoubtedly a common practice. Fortunately, I didn't use my teleconverter here, as there would be no time to remove it when the wing was briefly extended.

Page 154 Mute Swan
Tred Avon River, Maryland (January 1992) *Nikon F3, 600mm f4 lens, Fujichrome 100*

Mute Swans on Maryland's Eastern Shore are not the most challenging subject, especially when free corn is involved. A pair graced the creek by my parents' home and was more than happy to cruise by and avail themselves to handouts. After feeding they started to preen, contorting their bodies in all sorts of ways to do a thorough job. I intentionally shot the image tight to make it more of an abstract, isolating the twisted neck and rear. In the old days, one had to be very careful with metering bright white birds, which would tend to produce dark pictures without compensation. My current Nikon F5 can handle the situation with great consistency thanks to 3D matrix metering.

Photography Notes

Page 154 Northern Pintail
Newport Beach, California (January 2001) *Nikon F5, 600mm f4 lens with 2x TC, Kodak E100 VS*

A pool off the main channel at Newport Back Bay Ecological Reserve offers superb dabbling duck photography. When the tide drops, up to a few dozen pintail, teal (all three species), widgeon and mallards congregate in a shallow pool by the road. The birds are accustomed to seeing joggers, cyclists and kayakers. As such, they are remarkably acclimated and can be photographed at close range, a key to great duck photography. Waterfowl bathe, preen and rest here at different parts of the day during the winter months. I concentrated on this drake pintail perched in just a few inches of water. This frame shows off the beautiful edging of the flight feathers and a hint of metallic green.

Page 154 Short-billed Dowitcher
Estero Lagoon, Florida (January 2000) *Nikon F5, 600mm f4 lens with 1.4x TC, Kodak E100 VS*

Working the perimeter of Estero Lagoon at Fort Myers Beach is always an adventure as all kinds of waterbirds fish the shallows. Winter offers the most variety, especially with shorebirds like the dowitchers that breed far to the north. I came upon this belle an hour before sunset. Fortunately, the bird was alone, less likely to spook as it only takes one set of frightened eyes in a group to sound the alarm. I'm constantly impressed at how flexible birds are. Capturing extreme contortion on film is a challenge as these moments tend to be sudden and jerky. I was elated to see this dowitcher arch over the back and open the bill. The angle to the sun was just enough to catch sidelight.

Page 155 Common Goldeneye
Lake Merritt, California (January 2003) *Nikon F5, 600mm f4 lens with 2x TC, Kodak E100 VS*

By 2003 there were only a handful of waterfowl species that remained on my to-see list. Both goldeneyes were highly sought prizes. While photographing pelicans in La Jolla, we met a photographer who spoke highly of Lake Merritt in Oakland as a terrific place to see diving ducks. Since our trip ended in San Francisco, we would make time to scout out Lake Merritt. On our first visit, both species of goldeneye were visible, but far from shore. The second day was overcast, but I was determined to have a good shoot. Fortunately, a few Common Goldeneyes were preening close to the walkway. People are always jogging, biking and otherwise enjoying this urban park, so the ducks are fairly approachable.

Page 155 Great Egret
St. Augustine, Florida (April 1999) *Nikon F5, 600mm f4 lens, Fuji RMS (200)*

There are plenty of egret nests at the alligator farm, but the trick is to find one that offers a clean background. One nest at the top of the boardwalk was stellar, but there was only one precise angle between clustered branches that would do the trick. Over three days, I spent many hours on that exact spot to record the interplay of courting Great Egrets. While the mate was off looking for sticks to present, she guarded the prized nest. Preening can take place at anytime and I was in position when she started to manicure the nuptial plumes. The plumes play no role in flight as they are purely for decoration, spelling doom for their owners a century ago. Thousands were shot to festoon ladies' fancy hats.

Page 155 Anhinga
Ding Darling NWR, Florida (March 2001) *Nikon F5, 600mm f4 lens with 2x TC, Fuji Velvia 50*

Fortunately for bird lovers, Anhingas spend a lot of time preening and extending their wings to dry out after fishing. Their decreased buoyancy facilitates chasing down fish under water, but the plumage becomes easily waterlogged and requires additional maintenance. I shot several rolls of this male's full body and then popped on a 2x teleconverter to isolate the long, twisting neck against a simple blue background. The nickname "snake bird" seems apt. With all of the busy white streaking on the wings, it was critical to select a vantage point with a clean background. By stepping a few feet to my left, I was able to avoid a busy tangle of mangrove as a background.

Page 156 Brown Pelican
La Jolla, California (January 1999) *Nikon F5, 600mm f4 lens, Fuji Velvia 50*

This is one of those shots that I had in my head long before I had it on film. Artie and others had beautiful published shots of pelican head-throws and I was determined to create my own version. The best place to make such a shot is at the La Jolla cliffs by the Cave Shop. The shot would need to be taken in early winter when breeding adults display a deep crimson on their throat. There is little warning as to when a bird will initiate the accordion-style stretching of the elastic pouch. The key is to keep a resting bird in the frame, finger on the trigger while leaving plenty of room at the top for the stretch. For three mornings in a row, I intended to make the shot. This moment happened on the third day... isn't life grand!

Page 157 American White Pelicans
Freezeout Lake, Montana (June 1999) *Nikon F5, 600mm f4 lens with 1.4x TC, Kodak E100 VS*

This low-water angle was taken from my floating blind built from plywood, styrofoam and camouflage netting. I worked my way in from deeper water at a slow pace, so as not to disturb the roosting pelicans. I was able to select a beautiful green backdrop by carefully choosing my angle. I knew that Brown Pelicans did a neck-throw, but I wasn't sure if American White Pelicans would. I was delighted to see that they do share the maneuver. The stretch is more likely to happen after a bird has been resting for some time, so I simply waited patiently while the birds did their thing. With groups shots, it's best to avoid cutting off part of a bird when possible.

Page 157 Brown Pelican
Sarasota Bay, Florida (January 2000) *Nikon F5, 600mm f4 lens with 1.4x TC, Fuji Provia 100*

While heading to a pelican sanctuary near Sarasota, I happened upon a dock where fish were cleaned on a regular basis. I was not the only one drawn to such activity. Towards the end of the day, the birds perched on pilings after eating the tossed-out scraps. Since I am a big pelican fan, I stayed all afternoon instead of visiting the park that I had intended to see. This individual was sleeping when he untucked the bill and made a giant yawn followed by a neck-throw. I like how the photo illustrates the bill's flexibility. What endlessly entertaining creatures these pelicans are. I'm so enthralled by them that I hope to publish a photo book on pelicans one fine day.

Page 158 Wood Duck
Patterson Park, Maryland (October 2001) *Nikon F5, 600mm f4 lens, Kodak E100 VS*

Over a four year period, I probably shot as least 100 sequences of Wood Duck wing flaps. I threw out hard corn, a woodie favorite, which would sink and the woodies would have to dive for it. Upon surfacing, they habitually shake-off excess water to lighten the load. No matter how many flaps I shoot, no two frames look exactly the same, so I'm always game to try for more. I find this shot appealing due to the intricate feathering of the underwing and the iridescent colors on the head. For some cameras, this would be a metering challenge, but for Nikon's matrix metering I shoot at zero compensation in most situations. Due to the contrasty nature of VS film, highlight detail is lost on the white belly, but I can live with it.

Page 159 Common Loon
Bolsa Chica, California (January 1999) *Nikon F5, 600mm f4 lens with 1.4x TC, Fuji Velvia 50*

What a thrill to watch a loon feed right below the footbridge at Bolsa Chica. The water was clear enough to see it swim wildly after fish with great maneuverability. Perhaps shadows cast by the bridge, or its underwater structures, provided shelter for schooling fish. All sorts of waterbirds hunted right by us for three days of photographic bliss. Numerous dives would be made by the loon to yield one fish. Each time the bird caught something, there would be a wingflap, as if to celebrate the accomplishment. I kept my eye out for this winter-plumage loon resurfacing while scanning nearby grebes and ducks. Situations like this are great for autofocus as birds may pop up anywhere after a dive.

Page 159 Short-billed Dowitcher
Jamaica Bay, New York (August 1999) *Nikon F5, 600mm f4 lens with 1.4x TC, Kodak E100 VS*

Wild bird photography can be surprisingly easy at times, but it can also be a pain in the rump. Close-ups of shorebirds almost always fall into the latter category. Artie took us to a sheltered cove at Jamaica Bay early one August morning to work shorebirds that would be closer than normal due to the high tide. We inch-wormed across the beach (or was it a mudflat) to get close without spooking these difficult subjects. The hardest part was pivoting on knees and elbows with the big lens cradled in the hands... no tripods or monopods here. Once we got close to the waterline, the rest was relatively easy as a variety of species roosted, preened and bathed right in front of us. The lens mount was resting right on the ground. It's really messy work.

Page 160 Osprey
Tred Avon River, Maryland (July 2001) *Nikon F5, 600mm f4 lens with 2x TC, Kodak E100 VS*

An Osprey nesting platform was set up at my parents' home on Maryland's Eastern Shore in 1997. Two years later, when the towering chimney was rendered off-limits by strategic wire cages, we finally got to enjoy watching the Osprey nesting cycle up close. This male had a favorite perch for eating part of the catch before delivering it to the nest. I got permission from the neighbors to set up a blind on their dock for a good view. I waited several hours under the hot tarp and thought about quitting several times... "just another half-hour," I kept saying. He finally landed on the perch with a decapitated fish. When he raised his hindquarters, I knew what was coming (or going) and clicked the shutter before I saw the white stream.

Rhapsody In Blue

Page 161 Reddish Egret
Estero Lagoon, Florida
(November 2000) *Nikon
F5, 600mm f4 lens,
Fuji Provia 100*

This is the same bird
that appears on page
145 in a dramatic
charge. Before a rival entered his territory, he was feeding and resting. As there were no other birds at the shallow end of the lagoon, I focused my concentration on him
for nearly two hours. The instant he bent his legs and
arched the hindquarters, I put the lens on him. From
where I was, it was a tight fit into the frame, but I knew
there was no time to back up. I tend to shoot tighter
than a lot of folks, which can be a disadvantage when
the action heats up and extremities are elongated. Many
a shot has been thrown away because of a clipped bill,
wing or leg. I keep reminding myself that it's easier to
crop in than to recreate lost detail with Photoshop.

Page 162 Roseate Spoonbills
Merritt Island NWR, Florida
(April 1999) *Nikon F5, 600mm
f4 lens with 1.4x TC, Kodak
E100 VS*

I scheduled an extra day at
Merritt Island upon seeing spoonbills roosting next to the wildlife
drive. I got some decent shots
that first evening, but I sensed
the potential for much more.
These birds are creatures of habit and I figured they
would do it again tomorrow. My intuition paid off handsomely. I was treated to vigorous preening sessions
before they tucked in for the night. I chose a precise
angle to line up these three birds. You don't just get out
of the car and there's the perfect view of your subject...
you have to think about it. I stopped down to f11 to
increase depth-of-field. These birds are actually several
feet apart, compressed by a long telephoto.

Page 163 Stilt & Avocet
Palo Alto Baylands, California
(January 1999) *Nikon F5,
600mm f4 lens, Fuji Velvia 50*

Heading south to Monterey, we
scheduled a pit stop at the Palo
Alto Baylands below San
Francisco with the hopes of seeing a Clapper Rail. Shallow pools
near the visitor's center were
teeming with bird life and my
heart started to pound upon glimpsing Black-necked
Stilts and American Avocets resting together. The key to
this shot is a balanced composition. The out-of-focus avocet in the upper right is a nice contrast to the rest of
the picture. It's tempting to see a great subject and
start firing away without carefully considering the opti-
mal angle of view. Multiple birds layered against a struc-
tured background present a challenge to find that special vantage point.

**Page 164 Pelicans &
Commorants**
La Jolla, California
(January 2003) *Nikon
F100, 80-400mm f 4.5
lens, Kodak E100 VS*

This was my first shoot
at the pelican cliffs with-
out participating in a "Birds as Art" photo tour, yet I was
still learning from the master. After recording pelicans
with the big lens, Artie was inspired to do something different. I watched him and a few tour members work low
angles from ruts in the sandstone cliffs. By standing in
the deep crevices, they were able to get eye level shots
of the birds from just a few feet away. Not wanting to
miss out on the fun, yours truly popped on the short
zoom lens and went to work. It's extremely important in
situations like this to be considerate of others (in front
of you and behind) as you don't want to spook birds with
sudden movements while others are working.

**Page 166 Yellow-crowned
Night Heron**
Cape May, New Jersey (May
2001) *Nikon F5, 600mm f4 lens
with 2x TC, Kodak E100 VS*

A renowned bird photographer
from the Cape May area made
this shot possible thanks to his
generous spirit. When I met
Kevin in 1998 at the Cape May
Meadows, he offered to show me
some hotspots when I was in the area again. For three
years, I put out feelers among my contacts trying to find
a yellow-crowned colony that didn't require a blind. My
New Jersey associate heard of this interesting colony
next to a development and shared it with me. We photographed this pair of courting birds from step ladders
placed on a mowed lawn right in front of a townhouse.
A few years later, the colony was abandoned due to
increased development in the area, a real tragedy.

**Page 167 Black-legged
Kittiwake**
Middleton Island,
Alaska (July 2000)
*Nikon N90s, 300mm f4
lens, Kodak E100 VS*

Upon hearing there was
a Middleton Island in
Alaska covered with nesting seabirds, I was determined
to go. A year later, I met a photographer in Minnesota
who, against all odds, had been to this very island. I
called his contact, a field biologist, who graciously invited me to join them for their summer research with the
birds. This image was made from the stairs of an old
naval base radar tower that had been taken over by kittiwakes. The tower's ledges made for excellent nest sites.
Realizing what a unique opportunity this was, I spent
many hours in the tower enjoying the unobstructed view
of nesting kittiwakes. This particular nest was support-
ed by a metal beam that I cropped out.

Page 168 Northern Gannets
Cape St. Mary's, Newfoundland
(July 1999) *Nikon N90s, 28-
200mm f4.5 zoom lens,
Fuji Velvia 50*

After shooting several rolls of
nesting gannets atop Birdrock, I
was inspired to try something
different. It's so easy to go for
close-up shots with big lenses,
but it's important to zoom out
and show wildlife in a setting. I started to explore, moving away from the crowds for a distant view that illus-
trated the inspiring proportions of this rock tower, nearly 100 meters tall. I framed in some of the mainland
vegetation and distant Atlantic to give a sense of place.
This gannet colony, North America's second largest, spills
over onto adjacent mainland cliffs. Waves of fog will block
out the colony for long periods throughout the day,
adding to the mystique.

**Page 169 Northern
Gannets**
Cape St. Mary's,
Newfoundland (July
1999) *Nikon F5,
600mm f4 lens with
1.4 TC, Kodak E100 VS*

This project would not
have been possible without many photographers' tips.
Some information was gleaned from casual conversation
while most from research. My book collection included
Tim Fitzharris's *Nature Photography Hotspots* (Firefly
Books). Tim details a number of great birding trips
including the gannets on Newfoundland's Avalon
Peninsula. I booked a trip based on this recommendation.
At the end of a long clifftop trail is a viewing area that
overlooks the main gannet colony atop a huge seastack.
With a busy image of multiple birds such as this one, it
helps for the eye to have a focal point, like a bird flapping, to lead the viewer into the composition.

**Page 169 Common
Murres**
Cannon Beach, Oregon
(May 2001) *Nikon F5,
600mm f4 lens with 2x
TC, Fuji Provia 100*

From the glorious shores
of Cannon Beach, one
sees gigantic seastacks inundated with nesting seabirds.
However, they are a good distance offshore, at least a
couple hundred yards. One afternoon, I was feeling
adventurous and climbed my way up a cliff that over-
looked a dense colony of Common Murres. I was able to
find a vantage point, but it was still far away. Sensing
the job wasn't done, I returned the next morning. The
tide was very low, exposing what seemed like a mile of
sand that wasn't visible the day before. I walked out to
the new waterline where I was able to make this shot
with 1200 mm. The sliver of sky provides a visual break
in the composition.

Page 170 Snowy Egret
St. Augustine, Florida (April
1998) *Nikon F5, 600mm f4
lens, Fuji Provia 100*

Courting Snowy Egrets put on an
incredible show, a shower of luxurious plumes bristling with passion while their owners gurgle
strange calls that are imprinted
on my brain for life. The St.
Augustine Alligator Farm is a ter-
rific venue for viewing such vibrant life up close. The primary problem here is the dense vegetation. Getting a
clean shot without distracting branches and whitewashed
leaves is a huge challenge. This Snowy Egret popped up
on a branch where I could frame in a water background,
which photographed black upon exposing for the white
plumage. This image was made on an overcast day, which
can be ideal for many situations, especially while working bright white birds.

Page 171 White-cheeked Pintail
Pericles' Pond, Bahamas (May
2000) *Nikon F5, 600mm f4
lens, Fuji Provia 100*

Having never seen a wild
Bahamas Pintail before, I was
elated to be invited to a pond at
a private estate where over 100
ducks are fed daily. After 10 rolls of tight portraits, it
was time to be challenged. Every once in a while a drake
would perform a head-up, tail-up display to impress the
hens. The sequence lasts for only two or three seconds
with no preliminary sign to get you ready. The lens was
mounted on a Whimberly tripod head low to the ground.
With one hand on the camera and my eye just to the
side, I scanned the 30 birds right in front of me to find
an arched drake. Most sequences I missed because the
time interval was so short to compose and engage autofocus. The beautiful green speculum is normally tucked
away in resting posture.

Page 171 Red-winged Blackbird
Bear Branch Park, Maryland
(May 1994) *Nikon F3, 600mm
f4 lens with 1.4x TC,
Fuji Sensia 100*

My first attempt to photograph
calling Red-winged Blackbirds
was surprisingly easy. I returned
to a popular nature park in
Carroll County where I had seen
blackbirds in prior years. Cattails
lined each side of the boardwalk and a handful of birds
were displaying that morning. I staked out a spot on the
bank where I would have a direct line into a row of
uncluttered reeds. It's tough to see the black eye of this
species, yet proper angle to the sun will yield a twinkle
in the eye. This fellow would rotate among several
favorite perches and puff out the wings when calling for
a mate. By choosing a low angle, I was able to mix in
some blue sky in the background.

Photography Notes

Page 171 Blue-footed Booby
Isabel Island, Mexico (December 2000) *Nikon F100, 80-400 f4.5 lens, Kodak E100 VS*

Of all the wild courtship displays in the bird world, the Blue-footed Booby makes a strong case for "Best in Show." Tim Fitzharris describes a fabulous trip to a remote Mexican island covered with nesting seabirds. I made arrangements based on the information provided in *Nature Photography Hotspots* (Firefly Books, 1997). I spent two mornings with the Blue-footed Boobies at their lofty colony overlooking the Pacific Ocean. Nesting was in full swing by December, but only a handful of birds were doing the famous dance. In addition to the strong posturing, the birds will rock back and forth on alternating feet. The background is a little cluttered, but this is the best look I got of the dance.

Page 175 Eared & Red-necked Grebe
Freezeout Lake, Montana (June 1999) *Nikon F5, 600 f4 lens with 1.4x TC, Fuji Velvia 50*

Freezeout Lake hosts a huge colony of grebes, primarily the dainty Eared Grebe whose nests are easily spotted—clumps of harvested vegetation and bent reeds in open water. The large grebes tend to nest in the thick reedbeds. The challenge here is getting to the colony, a few hundred yards from shore. A floating blind is the only way in without disturbing the birds. The shallow lake features a soft bottom requiring me to inch forward on bent, bowed out knees most of the way out. What a smelly way to travel. Ninety minutes later, I was in the heart of grebe city. This Eared Grebe is rotating the eggs. Just behind me, I found a Red-necked Grebe peeking through the reeds.

Page 177 Western Sandpiper
Nome, Alaska (June 2001) *Nikon F5, 600 f4 lens with 1.4x TC, Fuji Provia 100*

Working shorebirds on arctic breeding grounds is some of the most arduous photography out there. Canvassing the tundra for several hours each day for a week, our group (led by Ralph Panoessa) found maybe ten nests of various species. All were skittish and tough to shoot. Towards the end of the trip, we found a Western Sandpiper with three tiny chicks just days old. I stayed with her for nearly two hours as she navigated the rugged terrain. Most of the time, you couldn't even spot them as they camouflage so well in the dense grass. Periodically, she laid down so the chicks could huddle under her warm belly. In this image, you can barely make out one chick underneath while one rests on her back.

Page 180 Bald Eagles
Middleton Island, Alaska (July 2000) *Nikon N90s, 24mm f2.8 lens, Kodak E100 VS*

Fascinated with raptors since childhood, I never dreamed that I would actually sit in an eagle's nest one day. In addition to thousands of nesting seabirds, Middleton Island hosts several Bald Eagle nests. This one was located atop a huge beach boulder at the far end of the island. I was given a general location for the nest, but it was the proverbial needle in a haystack. With divine intervention, I eventually found the nest and got great shots from the ground. It occurred to me that I could stack gathered driftwood at the base of the boulder to get a grip on the nest and hoist myself up. The chicks seemed surprisingly calm throughout the whole process. The adults watched from a cliff and never attacked.

Page 172 Yellow-head-ed Blackbird
Benton Lakes NWR, Montana (June 1999) *Nikon F5, 600 f4 lens with 1.4x TC, Kodak E100 VS*

This image is actually two frames printed side-by-side of the same bird just seconds apart. The left-hand page was flopped to simulate a face-off. The spread is intended to illustrate a variety of wing postures during a display. My efforts to document calling blackbirds from a floating blind on Freezeout Lake were unsuccessful, though the grebes were spectacular. I looked at a map and saw Benton Lakes NWR not too far away, so I ventured there for an afternoon. This was a sparsely vegetated refuge where the birds are typically far away. I finally encountered one male who was calling on my side of the canal. With cautious steps, I was able to close the gap.

Page 176 Common Loon
Three Mile Lake, Minnesota (June 2000) *Nikon F5, 600 f4 lens, Kodak E100 VS*

In addition to birds, I love to photograph all sorts of animals. I've had several great shoots at Minnesota Wildlife Connection, a game farm featuring trained wildlife models. I asked the proprietor if he knew of any loon lakes. I added a few days to the June trip for exploring some wild lakes of Minnesota in search of loons. I was hoping to see a bank nest, hidden in tall grasses. On the second lake explored near Sandstone, we canoed for two hours and I was giving up hope when we came upon this open-water nest. The bird was shy and we had to pull back. The next day, I canoed out to the nest with a friend and she deposited me on the shore. When she backed off the canoe, the loon returned to incubate.

Page 178 Anhinga
Anhinga Trail, Florida (February 2001) *Nikon F100, 80-400 f4.5 lens, Kodak E100 VS*

I heard about great opportunities for nesting Anhingas along the Anhinga Trail in Everglades National Park, but we only found one very distant nest on our first visit in 1999. Two years later, I was delighted to find several nests close to the boardwalk. This one was just ten feet away. Nevertheless, the nest and its three precarious nestlings were well-concealed behind branches. Every time a bird moved, there was a new branch in the way. For three mornings in a row, I stood vigil. At feeding time, the nestlings are very active and stretch out. All the elements seemed to come together for this one frame. I added fill flash at minus-one compensation to open up some shadow details.

Page 182 Black-legged Kittiwakes
Middleton Island, Alaska (July 2000) *Nikon N90s, 24mm f2.8 lens, Fuji Provia 100*

The old radar tower on Middleton Island offers a unique, intimate view of nesting kittiwakes and cormorants. Cubicles accessed by a trap door were installed by biologists for easy viewing and banding during the nesting cycle. The view simulated looking through the rock wall anchoring the nest. The one-way glass panel could be slid up, yielding a six inch square opening just wide enough to fit a wide-angle lens through with a small macro-flash mounted on the hot shoe. The moment this parent returned, I snapped the frame. Fortunately, the beautiful red mouth was open. These nests are intentionally small to prevent larger predatory gulls from landing.

Page 174 Clark's Grebe
Freezeout Lake, Montana (June 1999) *Nikon F5, 600 f4 lens with 2x TC, Fuji Velvia 50*

I secured permission to deploy a floating blind to photograph nesting grebes at this remote wildlife management area north of Great Falls. I had no blueprints for such a blind. Common sense told me to sandwich a block of Styrofoam with plywood and secure four corner posts to support camouflage material and branches draped over crossbeams. I did not calculate buoyancy... it would either sink or swim. I saw several swimming Clark's Grebes, but I still hoped for a nest. On the second day, I poked around the reedbeds and came upon this lovely incubating adult. She was nervous, so I only moved inches at a time to get a clean shot of her. I intentionally framed the eye with the reeds.

Page 177 White-tailed Tropicbird
Great Inagua, Bahamas (May 2000) *Nikon N90s, 200 f4 macro lens, Fuji Provia 100*

Our guide for the flamingo colony told of a great beach for nesting tropicbirds, which I was dying to photograph. We were dumped off on a remote corner of the island and were handed a bottle of insect repellent. We would be picked up three hours later. Little did we know that one of the greatest mosquito attacks of the century was about to take place and our only refuge was the water, where they would still bite us unless we fully submerged. I climbed down a small cliff face hoping to find tropicbird nests in rocky crevices. I had to abandon my search as the footing became precarious. Exploring a different part of the beach, I poked my head in a cave and there she was hunkered down. My flash saved the day.

Page 179 Great Blue Heron
Venice Rookery, Florida (January 2000) *Nikon F5, 600mm f4 lens with 1.4x TC, Fuji Velvia 50*

It's easy to see why the Venice Rookery is so crowded. Great photo ops at close range await for several months out of the year. I've been there three times and each visit has offered up wonderful and unique moments. I also enjoy talking to fellow nature photographers and sharing information. There's plenty of variety to keep things interesting. One nest may feature mating birds while ten feet away large chicks are being fed. When a parent lands for the morning feeding, things get crazy. The chicks peck vigorously at the adult's bill to encourage regurgitation. For this sequence, I probably shot 50 frames in a just a few minutes and every frame had a slightly different look.

Page 183 Glaucous-winged Gull
Middleton Island, Alaska (July 2000) *Nikon F5, 600mm f4 lens with 1.4x TC, Kodak E100 VS*

With upwards of 20,000 kittiwakes and other seabirds, Middleton Island is sure to draw the attention of predatory birds like eagles and large gulls to cull the bounty. I found this kittiwake chick near our campsite. The body was still warm, but it had expired. Perhaps it had fallen out of a nest when jostling with siblings. Its wounds indicated a Glaucous-winged Gull had been picking on it. I placed the chick on a nearby cliff and stood back, waiting for a gull to land and finish the meal. There is no point in nutrients going to waste. Within 15 minutes, a big Glacous-winged Gull landed and claimed its prize. Such is the unforgiving circle of life at a seabird colony.

Rhapsody In Blue

Page 183 Glaucous-winged Gull
Middleton Island, Alaska (July 2000) *Nikon N90s, 105mm f2.8 lens, Kodak E100 VS*

Having my fill of puffin and kittiwake shots, I decided to roam the vast beaches in search of elusive shorebirds. If I was lucky, I might turn up an oystercatcher nest. My wanderings eventually yielded a gull chick anxiously awaiting the return of its parents. There was no ground nest in the immediate vicinity, as the chick was large enough to be exploring its surroundings. Eventually it settled down in a small patch of wildflowers. Fortunately, I had brought along my 105mm macro lens, as I could get very close to the chick. Roaming around this haunting outpost in the Gulf of Alaska, it was very sweet to encounter such precious moments, a profusion of life in this chilled Eden.

Page 184 American White Pelican
Lake Manitoba, Canada (June 1998) *Nikon N90s, 105mm f2.8 lens, Fuji Sensia 100*

I was in a hurry to set up the tent blind on this remote island in Lake Manitoba. I hired a birding guide to provide access to this huge colony of pelicans, gulls and cormorants. Over a hundred adult pelicans took flight upon our arrival, alighting on massive eight-foot wingspans. It felt like a scene from Jurassic Park. While scouting for a spot to set up the blind, I came across this tiny orange chick just days old. There were many other chicks on the island, but they were all downy-white and much larger. As soon as I entered my blind, the guide and captain anchored offshore and the pelicans reunited with their chicks for a blissful shoot.

Page 185 Canada Goose, Ring-billed Gull
Lake Manitoba, Canada (June 1998) *Nikon N90s, 105mm f2.8 lens, Fuji Provia 100*

En route to the large pelican colony, we made a few pitstops at various islands to search for nesting birds. One island featured a small heron rookery, which we discovered to be abandoned. Though the colony had moved on, some geese had found the accommodations to their liking. It didn't take long to see what all the fuss was about. Several bright yellow goslings scrambled over broken eggshells while a fresh hatchling held tight. This was my first goose nest and I was on cloud nine. Another small island hosted a huge colony of gulls. Hundreds of Ring-billed Gulls swirled overhead as we landed. Walking around, we had to be very careful not to step on any little ones.

Page 186 Black Skimmer
Ocean City, Maryland (June 1994) *Nikon FE2, 105mm f2.8 lens, Fuji Velvia 50*

With *Maryland's Great Outdoors* (1996), I dove headfirst into the world of nature photography. The Maryland Department of Natural Resources really reached out to me, especially when it came to the waterbirds. I got permission to set up blinds within sensitive nesting areas and I was able to accompany field biologists as they monitored various colonies. One exciting place is easily viewed from the bridge that lands you in old Ocean City, a bustling summer resort town on the Atlantic Ocean. On this fragile low sandy island surrounded by recreational boaters, a handful of species nests each summer, including the Black Skimmer. I was nervous walking on the beach with such well-camouflaged eggs and chicks.

Page 188 White-tailed Tropicbird
Great Inagua, Bahamas (May 2000) *Nikon F5, 600mm f4 lens with 1.4x TC, Fuji Provia 100*

Upwards of a dozen tropicbirds were dancing about the skies near a beach where cliff crevices would safeguard the next generation. The nesting season was in full swing and courtship flight at a peak. The beach hooked around to a point where I would be closest to the action, so I set up there and hoped to document my first ever tropicbird. The birds were looping past the cliffs, but usually at a great distance. Eventually, I saw two birds flying together, but too distant to shoot. I hoped for a close fly-by, which finally appeared after another 100 mosquito bites. At long last, two birds merged together right in front of the cliff and I had my golden opportunity. This image is cropped in a bit. Fortunately, the grain on new slide films is super-tight.

Page 188 Arctic Terns
Churchill, Canada (June 1998) *Nikon F5, 600mm f4 lens with 1.4x TC, Fuji Provia 100*

Our guide, Moose Peterson, took the group to ponds close to town where a variety of birds were staging, most notably the Arctic Tern. An occasional bird would pass by with a fish in its bill, showing off his catch. It looked like he was teasing potential mates with the treat. One bird with an attractive fish paraded around the pond for a good while. Eventually, he landed on a rock where another bird was perched. Having the second bird in the frame, presumably a female, helps to illustrate the story of tern courtship. The light was gloomy for most of the trip, but that didn't prevent me from trying to make the most of the situation. Don't be discouraged by less-than-perfect weather.

Page 189 Great Blue Heron
Venice Rookery, Florida (January 2000) *Nikon F5, 600mm f4 lens with 1.4x TC, Kodak E100 VS*

My favorite shooting at the Venice Rookery is when sticks are brought into the nest. The setting is perfect for morning flight shots of Great Egrets and Great Blue Herons. The trees on the island are relatively short, yielding a clean blue sky background when the waders approach with legs dropped. Once a bird lands, the mate tending the nest will get excited and puff out the plumes. Great Blue Herons also elongate the neck and point skyward for just a moment before grabbing the stick away from their partner. I must have shot at least twenty stick ceremonies at this nest over a three-day shoot. During the breeding season they don Carolina blue lores by the eyes.

Page 189 Hooded Mergansers
Druid Hill Park, Maryland (November 2002) *Nikon F5, 600mm f4 lens with 2x TC, Fuji Provia 100*

Every fall, nearly two dozen wild Hooded Mergansers visit the waterfowl lake at The Baltimore Zoo and stay until the first freeze. I tried to get close-ups from a floating blind, which I got permission to use, but I couldn't fool them. Plan B was to stand on the bank and be as still as possible and hopefully the birds would get used to me. I was delighted one day to see courtship, the spirited, crested drakes dancing circles around the coy hen. Now I knew the shot that I wanted for the book. One or two shoots later, birds were swimming maybe 150 feet away when the males flared up as a hen approached. What a great drama in nature to behold, especially in Baltimore City.

Page 190 Western Grebes
Freezeout Lake, Montana (June 1999) *Nikon F5, 600mm f4 lens with 1.4x TC, Fuji Velvia 50*

This was the shot in my mind's eye that inspired the adventure to Freezeout Lake. Most of the grebes that I saw were already on eggs and I thought that I was too late for the courtship dance. The second day, I saw one pair rush across the lake at a distance in poor light. On the third day paddling around with my floating blind, I discovered this pair swimming through my left porthole. Without warning they burst into motion maybe fifty feet away. Quick reflexes saved the day... with my left hand, I grabbed the blind and swung it around 45 degrees while my right hand went for the camera balanced on a Whimberly head. I hastily found the birds in the viewfinder and shot while panning.

Page 192 Mallards
Patterson Park, Maryland (May 2000) *Nikon F5, 600mm f4 lens, Fuji Provia 100*

I set out a variety of logs at this popular lake in Baltimore City for the resident Wood Ducks to perch on. Two woodie hens had small broods and I was waiting for them to haul out. Along came a Mallard with a single duckling. Just a few days earlier, I saw her with a half-dozen protégés... I suspect the snapping turtles were doing well in the park. It's important to keep your eye in the viewfinder, as this quack by mom only happened once that session and it lasted maybe three seconds. Normally, the ducks don't protest your proximity as they readily accept handouts from park-goers throughout the year. I can understand her being overprotective of her last surviving offspring.

Page 193 Mute Swans
Tred Avon River, Maryland (June 2000) *Nikon F5, 300mm f2.8 with 1.4x TC, Kodak E100 VS*

Photographing from a kayak is a great experience. You can paddle in very shallow water, maneuver quickly and stay low to the horizon. I knew that swans nested on this creek, so I cruised the perimeter with the hope of a close encounter. Momma was very nervous when I found her at the end of the creek, which opened up into a secluded cove. I paralleled her as her signets followed close behind near the shoreline. Perhaps an hour passed before I could get close enough to attempt shots. I positioned myself just ahead of these fast swimmers to allow time to gather the camera and set up. Once the birds have passed, swimming away, the image is not as engaging.

Page 193 Pacific Loon
Anchorage, Alaska (July 2000) *Nikon F5, 600mm f4 lens with 1.4x TC, Kodak E100 VS*

For my big trip to Middleton Island in the Gulf of Alaska, I added a few days to my stopover in Anchorage to take advantage of local birds. My contact at the Fish and Wildlife Service spoke of a few lakes in town that had nesting loons, and I was game. Her friend with a canoe volunteered to help me get some shots, as I knew that if I was confined to walking the shoreline, my opportunities would be limited. A portion of this lake was roped off for swimming, so the birds are used to people here. The light was poor that day and there was no depth-of-field, a tough proposition when photographing multiple birds. After a while, the loons acclimated to us and I simply waited for the three to line up for a nice family portrait.

Photography Notes

Page 194 Osprey
Tred Avon River, Maryland (July 2000) *Nikon F5, 600mm f4 lens with 1.4x TC, Fuji Sensia 100*

Since childhood, I have felt a kinship with the Osprey. No matter how many times I have photographed them, I can never have too many pictures of this friendly raptor. When Osprey nested on a platform at my parents' Eastern Shore home, it was a dream come true. I would have total access to document my favorite bird of the Chesapeake Bay. The nest was best positioned for afternoon light, so I would set up my rig under a glorious maple tree at 2 or 3 p.m. and wait for dad to bring in dinner. Once he dropped it off the female would rip off tidbits and feed the two chicks. I selected this frame because there is a lot going on, and the composition balances well with wings on top and sticks below.

Page 194 Osprey
Estero Lagoon, Florida (March 1999) *Nikon F5, 600mm f4 lens with 1.4x TC, Fuji Provia 100*

Of my many visits to Estero Lagoon at Ft. Myers Beach, I've seen so many incredible moments with the birds that I could do a small book on the place. Opportunities abound in this most unusual set-up... a long, shallow lagoon that you can wade in. Things can happen pretty quickly, so I shoot on a monopod to be ready in moments. I saw a dot on the horizon that looked more and more unusual as it approached. I soon realized that it was a large bird carrying a stick, cutting across my path. Autofocus locked onto the white belly and I was able to make several sharp frames as the raptor passed. I can't recall a trip here where I didn't see and photograph Osprey. They are just as common in Florida as in the Chesapeake Bay, my home turf.

Page 195 Osprey
Ocean City, Maryland (June 1994) *Nikon F3, 600mm f4 lens with 1.4x TC, Fuji Velvia 50*

I saw this nest while driving to a market and made a note to scout it out the next day. I found one spot in a residential area where I could be fairly close to the nest without trespassing. Facing west, I decided to return that evening, and if lucky the sun would be setting somewhere near the background. As it turned out, the sun set right behind the nest that second week of June. One bird was already in the nest and the mate flew in just moments before this image was made. All the elements were there, but one key would complete the shot—profiled heads with hooked bills. Both birds were constantly changing their angle of view, but there was a moment when they profiled simultaneously.

Page 196 Eared Grebe
Freezeout Lake, Montana (June 1999) *Nikon F5, 600mm f4 lens with 1.4x TC, Kodak E100 VS*

Of the nearly 100 Eared Grebes that I saw at this huge colony on Freezeout Lake, I found only two pair with young. Most of the birds were on eggs or beginning to build. This is one of the great things about working colonial waterbirds—they don't all start the process at exactly the same time, so you may witness various stages of the nesting cycle at any given time. I stayed with this pair for an hour and was able to make several wonderful shots of the babies on mom's back. Dad would dive for several minutes at a time for tiny morsels to feed the chicks. There was a third chick nestled in the feathers that you cannot see in this frame. Chicks can clamp down on a parent's feathers to ride out a dive.

Page 197 Red-necked Grebe
Anchorage, Alaska (June 2001) *Nikon F5, 600mm f4 lens with 2x TC, Fuji Provia 100*

I heard of some lakes around Anchorage that hosted nesting Red-necked Grebes, so I added two days to my Nome trip before flying home. I scouted four lakes and two had nests that were shootable from shore. I made a floating blind for this nest to get extra close, but the birds were swimming for most of the day with their two chicks. I didn't realize that they would return to the nest for resting, so I'm glad that I stuck around to finish off the day shooting from the bank. This chick is much larger than its sibling hidden from view. When it scampered for a safe, warm resting spot, I felt that all of my hard work was finally paying off. I waited patiently for special moments such as mom's bill turning to her youngster.

Page 198 Greater Flamingoes
Great Inagua, Bahamas (May 2000) *Nikon F5, 600mm f4 lens with 2x TC, Fuji Provia 100*

My big shoot with the flamingo colony did not go as planned. My heart was set on adults standing atop their mud huts, tiny nestlings huddled below. The timing of hatching varies from year-to-year. I learned after two hours of hiking over treacherous salt lakes that we were a few weeks late for my dream shoot. The chicks were now big enough to be wandering about. I didn't know that they grouped together in a massive nursery while the adults feed. The birds in this protected, remote sanctuary were suspicious and I had to shoot from a great distance. There's tremendous compression at 1200mm as the birds look like they are crawling on top of each other, but they are spaced out to some degree.

Page 200 American Coots & Lesser Scaup
Freezeout Lake, Montana (June 1999) *Nikon F5, 600mm f4 lens, Fuji RMS (200)*

After getting my fill of nesting grebes over three days of great shooting, I was feeling adventurous on my last day and decided to paddle my floating blind into the reeds. My first surprise was a huge muskrat hauled out, munching on some tender shoots. Just around the corner I discovered baby coots, adorable with red bills and yellow-orange down. Six young were milling about the reeds as the parents delivered food maybe 12 feet in front of my blind. Later on that day, I walked the shoreline and accidentally flushed a trio of cute ducklings. The nearest adult bird was a Scaup hen, so I assumed they belonged to her. Within three seconds, the yellow puffballs disappeared into the reeds.

Page 200 Great Egrets
St. Augustine, Florida (April 1999) *Nikon F5 600mm f4 lens, Fuji Provia 100*

On this particular trip to the St. Augustine Alligator Farm, this egret nest was the best to photograph, almost eye-level with the boardwalk that traverses the big alligator pond. Over three days, I spent many hours standing vigil with this family of Great Egrets. Every time a bird re-positioned in the nest, there was a new opportunity for an interesting composition. The shot that I really wanted appears on page 267, but this moment was a welcomed surprise. The bigger chick's personality is very evident as he demands another regurgitated meal, but his efforts are in vain as mom has already emptied her crop. Soon her mate returned with a fresh pot of fish. The cascading plumes on the back will be shed shortly after nesting.

Page 201 Killdeer
Lake Manitoba, Canada (June 1998) *Nikon F5, 600mm f4 lens, Fuji Provia 100*

I hired a birding guide near Lake Manitoba in Central Canada to get me close to a host of waterbirds, especially nesting white pelicans. On one of our excursions, he took me to a friend's farm with several ponds. We canoed around, but the grebes ducked in the reeds. On foot, we were able to see lots of Canada Geese and a few shorebirds. We heard the call of an alarmed Killdeer nearby and started searching. Eventually, a single chick popped up and ran around. I tracked him in the field as he ventured off to the adjacent pond. Every once in a while he would stop to get his bearings—a fleeting opportunity to freeze the motion of a speedy youngster. A blue-water background was a bonus.

Page 201 Mew Gull
Anchorage Lakes, Alaska (June 2001) *Nikon F5, 600mm f4 lens, Fuji Provia 100*

After returning from Nome, where eight out of nine days were totally overcast, I was anxious to expose some film with several hours of daylight left. I had never been so glad to see the sun shine and I raced off to Potter Marsh, where I had a good chance of seeing birds. Alas, Mew Gulls swimming around and a few diving ducks in the reeds... I was coming out of a funk from light depravation. Right by the parking lot at the marsh were a trio of Mew Gull chicks. They were not particularly shy nor were the parents alarmed, so I figured that people feed the birds here at this popular sanctuary. I hung with the fledglings as they moved about the grass; eventually one perched on a rock and yawned.

Page 201 Sandhill Cranes
Lake Kissimmee, Florida (April 1999) *Nikon F5, 600mm f4 lens with 1.4x TC, Kodak E100 VS*

While cruising close to shore in a chartered airboat, I noticed a pair of Sandhill Cranes feeding in a pasture. I sensed that some youngsters were underfoot, which I confirmed with binoculars. I asked the captain to deposit us on the shore. The suspicious adults retreated with their little ones not far behind. I had never seen crane chicks before and I was hopeful of making pictures. I followed the cranes as they wandered the pasture, but the chicks got lost in the grass. We launched a search and eventually found these two huddled together. With 840mm of lens, I could shoot at a respectable distance while the adult watched the proceedings. When we backed off, one adult returned.

Page 202 Parakeet Auklets
Pribilof Islands, Alaska (July 1998) *Nikon N90s, Tokina 400mm f5.6 lens, Fuji Sensia 100*

At the opposite end of St. Paul Island from where you stay, I recall a steep grassy slope where we hiked each day to access rugged cliffs loaded with seabirds. With all the camera gear in tow, the ascent really took the wind out of me. About half-way up, I stopped to take in the view while catching my breath. I noticed a pair of Parakeet Auklets perched on a crag. My initial response was to grab the 600mm lens and teleconverters for close-ups, but the scene was so spectacular that I went for the habitat shot. I framed in a crashing wave to provide a sense of place while balancing the dark tones on the right side of the composition. I was careful not to center the birds.

Rhapsody In Blue

Page203 Atlantic Puffins
Cape Bonavista, Newfoundland (July 1999) *Nikon N90s, 600mm f4 lens with 2x TC, Kodak E100 VS*

I had a delightful stay at the quaint town of Trinity where a renowned whale researcher, Dr. Peter Beamish, runs an inn with his wife. I asked if he could suggest a good place to photograph puffins and he recommended Cape Bonavista. I was elated to hear that puffins would be maybe fifty feet away at Cape Bonavista, a dream come true. The next day, I found the puffins all right, but at the closest point I could be, they were at least 300 feet away... not exactly portrait range. Though very disappointed, I decided to make the most of it and tried for flight shots when occasional birds pased by. Eventually, a group of puffins came out of their burrows on a distant grassy slope for a good shot.

Page205 Great Blue Heron
Venice Rookery, Florida (February 2001) *Nikon F5, 600mm f4 lens with 2x TC, Kodak E100 VS*

The Venice Rookery reminds me of the Superbowl, lots of shooters lined up on the sidelines (bank) with big lenses, shooting away at the non-stop action. During the winter and spring months, a few dozen waders—mostly Great Egrets and Great Blue Herons—nest on the island's dense trees and shrubs. This morning, I was concentrating on one particular Great Egret displaying at the nest. Several feet below, I noticed this duo of fledgling Great Blue Herons who were quite mobile at this stage. I waited until their heads were profiled in a sliver of blue sky accented by red berries. Birds are front lit in the morning and artsy silhouettes can be attempted in the afternoon.

Page208 Pectoral Sandpiper
Barrow, Alaska (June 2000) *Nikon F5, 600mm f4 lens, Kodak E100 VS*

The tundra of the far north is a bleak and challenging place to photograph birds. There's lots of walking over inhospitable terrain with heavy equipment. When you find a bird to photograph, whether it be a shorebird, loon, duck or songbird, they are usually skittish. I saw many Pectoral Sandpipers in Barrow that trip, but they always wanted to keep a good distance away from me. This day was proving to be a bust. A pair of Red-throated Loons proved elusive subjects, and I fell in a pit of cold ooze, almost ruining my gear. On the way back to the road, the sun broke out and I hoped to finally expose some film. A sandpiper popped up on a grassy mound and seemed willing to work with me.

Page210 Black Skimmers
Cape May, New Jersey (October 2001) *Nikon F5, 600mm f4 lens, Fuji Provia 100*

I find that it is very helpful to start the day with clear intention. This autumn morning in Cape May, our instructional photo tour group assembled on the beach before sunrise. I positioned myself behind a flock of skimmers and terns, making the rising sun my background. Ideally, I hoped for a flying bird silhouetted against a big, orange sun. My dream shot did not materialize, but I noticed that the skimmers were returning close to where they had just been roosting. When crashing waves rolled up the beach, they shimmered bright orange, a wonderful backdrop for flying birds. For this frame, I did manual override on the autofocus as the lens can get confused when birds pass the selected sensors.

Page204 Sora
Wakodahatchee Wetlands, Florida (March 1999) *Nikon F5, 600mm f4 lens, Fuji Velvia 50*

I'm so thankful that a friendly bird photographer named, oddly enough, Bill Smylie, told us about Wakodahatchee Wetlands, a water treatment facility near West Palm Beach. The heavily vegetated ponds are a waterbird mecca with never a dull moment. I've consistently seen Soras here, a diminutive and typically shy rail that makes for an elusive photographic subject. Walking the boardwalk, I noticed this little fellow feeding and decided it was worth a try despite the dense cover. When feeding, many birds are jerky and unpredictable, making it a challenge to freeze on film. This Sora had just found a tidbit to eat, a reason to pause at the water's edge. An instant later he was off, lost in the jungle.

Page206 Assorted Wading Birds
Loxahatchee NWR, Florida (March 1999) *Nikon F5, 400mm f3.5 lens, Fuji Provia 100*

A year before this picture was made, I ventured to Loxahatchee and found just a handful of birds along the main impoundment. On this visit in 1999, we were shocked at how the large lake from last year was little more than a puddle. The surviving fish were now concentrated in a shallow ditch. It was a feeding frenzy, the likes of which I've never seen before. Every few seconds, another fish was pulled out from this death trap. Wading birds typically feed at a distance from each other; this was quite the anomaly. By the time we found this spot, the sun had been up for three hours... not ideal light for white birds. I underexposed the film to help preserve some detail in the highlights.

Page209 King Eider
Barrow, Alaska (June 2000) *Nikon F5, 600mm f4 lens with 2x TC, Fuji Provia 100*

This is my favorite duck of the whole five-year project, the one that I traveled 5,000 miles to see in the wild, and the one that helped renew my faith in an immensely generous God. Our first three days in Barrow turned up a few Common Eiders, a pair of Stellar's Eiders, a rumored Spectacled Eider, but no sighting of a King Eider. On the second to last day, a chance conversation struck up with a van of birdwatchers yielded a tip that sounded too good to be true. There he was in all of his glory, swimming in a tiny pool of melt-water at the edge of a frozen lake. That day and the next, I shot nearly fifty rolls of this one duck that was remarkably tolerant. Sculpted ice rimmed the pond... what a background.

Page211 King Rail
Cape May, New Jersey (October 1998) *Nikon F5, 600mm f4 lens, Fuji Sensia 100*

The Cape May Meadows were wonderful during my first shoot in 1998. The water level was just right for a host of wading birds to reap the bounty. Having my fill of egrets and yellowlegs, I took a stroll to see who else was lurking in the shadows. A few photographers had discovered a rail hidden in the tangle. I caught a glimpse through the dense marsh reeds lining the footpath. I realized that if I wanted good shots of this new species, I needed to be on the other side of the reeds... I found a small gap in the bushes and pushed through to the pond's edge where there was just a sliver of land to set up on a monopod. Moments later, the King Rail emerged from the cover and waded across a shallow ditch.

Page205 Common Moorhen
Ding Darling NWR, Florida, (March 1999) *Nikon F5, 600mm f4 lens, Fuji Provia 100*

I've spent many hours walking the cross-dike at Ding Darling on Sanibel Island. It can be very quiet or full of action depending on a number of variables. Usually, one sees a handful of wading birds and a few diving cormorants and grebes. This morning featured a Reddish Egret at close range, a real treat. When the bird flew off, I walked patiently to see if anything else might show up. In a tangle of mangrove, my eye caught the movement of a small drab bird with a flashy red shield on the forehead. I saw the moorhen approaching this cluster of roots and positioned the lens for a dynamic habitat shot. I tried my best to keep a few of the green leaves in the top of the frame.

Page208 Glaucous-winged Gull
Middleton Island, Alaska (July 2000) *Nikon F5, 600mm f4 lens with 1.4x TC, Kodak E100 VS*

It was a wonderful adventure to explore the vast, rocky beaches of Middleton Island. Once a military base, the privately owned island is now left for the birds. After working the puffins, kittiwakes and eagles pretty hard, I decided to stroll the beaches to see if anything else popped up. The island hosts a strong population of the ground-nesting Glaucous-winged Gull. When I came upon this gull perched on driftwood, framed by pink fireweed, I felt that I had discovered something very special. The log's whitewash indicates that it is a favored perch. On overcast days like this one, I prefer to use the Kodak VS film, which warms up muted tones, especially greens.

Page210 Sanderling
Stone Harbor, New Jersey (October 1998) *Nikon F5, 600mm f4 lens, Fuji Sensia 100*

Every time I visited the Jersey Shore for bird photography, I've been pleasantly surprised. On this fall afternoon in 1998, the beach looked very typical, a handful of gulls and terns working the surf zone while pods of little sandpipers canvassed the wet sand. I tried for running shots of Sanderlings with modest success until the group settled down for the night. Working a group of clustered, sleeping Sanderlings, I noticed this lone bird amidst a stretch of marooned clams. To make the most of it, I dropped to my knees and compressed the scene from a low vantage point. I also made sure that a clean patch of sand framed the bird's head.

Page212 Ruddy Turnstone & Red Knot
Cape May, New Jersey (May 1998) *Nikon F5, 600mm f4 lens with 1.4x TC, Fuji Velvia 50*

I distinctly remember the thrill of driving off to the Delaware Bay in the spring of 1998 for my first big shorebird shoot. I started out on the Delaware side and drove to Cape May that afternoon. I checked out several noted shorebird viewing areas, including Reed's Beach, but posted signs asked that people not go on the beach. I finally found a secluded beach with large flocks of turnstones and knots and maintained a healthy buffer, so as not to spook them. I noticed how flocks would periodically alight... now that would be a shot to try for. I framed in these feeding birds at the bottom and left plenty of open area once they took flight. Fortunately, the birds filled out the frame for a balanced composition.

Photography Notes

Page214 Common Loon
Three Mile Lake, Minnesota
(June 2000) *Nikon N90s,
200mm f4 lens, Kodak E100 VS*

After two days of searching in vain, I was delighted to find this beautiful loon nest at the far corner of a popular fishing lake not far from Sandstone. That morning, I shot several rolls from the bank of the loon incubating its eggs. Later that day, we returned to try for some different angles. I was able to shoot with a 600mm lens from the canoe on still water. Most loon nests are built on a lake's bank, concealed by dense grass. This nest is constructed of pond lily tubers and other gathered vegetation. I had a few frames left on a roll and decided to do a habitat portrait with the short lens. I was saddened to learn that a few days later the nest had been washed out by storm waves.

Page215 Trumpeter Swan
Hennepin Parks, Minnesota
(September 1999) *Nikon N90s,
80-200 f2.8 lens, Fuji Velvia 50*

Hiking down to the lake that morning, I thought I was in a movie. The sun was just coming up, lighting autumn foliage above mist rising from the lake, home to a family of six Trumpeter Swans. Initially, I did tight family portraits with the 600mm lens. Fortunately, I brought along my 80-200 zoom. I made time to do scenics featuring the maples on the distant shore. When doing group shots, it is important to watch the juxtaposing birds to avoid problems like two heads overlapping. Sunbeams were shooting narrowly through gaps in the trees, lighting up the birds unevenly for a spotlight effect. I was glad to see that this frame included illumination of the right-hand adult.

Page216 Gulls & Terns
Mustang Island, Texas
(March 2000) *Nikon
F5, 28-200 f4.5 lens,
Fuji Provia 100*

After a good morning shoot in Corpus Christi, we had a few hours to kill and looked at the map for inspiration. I saw Mustang Island State Park, less than an hour's drive away. We checked some jetties for shorebirds, but the light was very bright and it was getting hot. Heading back to the parking lot, we came upon a large group of gulls and terns roosting on the beach. I noticed the waves in the background and waited for the flock to take wing. Mixed in with the Laughing Gulls are Royal Terns with orange bills. If you search closely, there are two Forster's Terns (completely black bill) and two Sandwich Terns (black bill with yellow tip). I did not realize this until a year later when examining the slides.

Page217 Snowy Plover
Bolivar Flats, Texas
(March 2000) *Nikon F5,
600mm f4 lens with 1.4x TC,
Fuji Provia 100*

Having seen many published waterbird photos from Bolivar Flats, I was very eager to check out this coastal Texas hotspot. Walking down the beach toward the point, I saw scads of birds lined up on the sandbars, including a large flock of pelicans and avocets. I was really hoping to photograph the avocets, but they were spooky, even from a great distance away. As many birdwatchers come here, I did not want to take the chance of flushing the flock, so I held back. Every once in a while, small shorebirds would appear and dart across the sand. I was able to photograph two Piping Plovers and a Snowy Plover, a new species for me. By maintaining a respectable distance, this bird allowed me to tag along as he worked the beach.

Page217 American Bittern
Brazos Bend Park,
Texas (March 2000)
*Nikon F5, 600mm f4
lens, Kodak E100 VS*

This same bird appears on page 16 eating a crayfish. The write-up on page 243 describes how we came to meet. Once I had the elusive bird in my sights, I spent the next two hours patiently observing his movements. Since I became interested in birds during the early 1990's, I've only seen six American Bitterns in the wild—two in Maryland, two in Florida, and two in Texas. My success rate with the smaller Least Bittern tallies only three, all in Florida. It's very unusual to see a bittern fully exposed like this one. Over the course of two hours, I shot maybe six rolls of various angles as he stalked the wet ditch for food. We were very close, but it never seemed to bother the bird.

Page217 Whooping Crane & Roseate Spoonbill
Aransas NWR, Texas
(March 2000) *Nikon F5,
600mm f4 lens with
1.4x TC, Fuji Provia 100*

My big hope for the trip was to see Whooping Cranes. The place to go is Aransas NWR, a vast swath of tidal marsh that represents the species last winter stronghold. Thanks to an intensive captive breeding program, Whooping Cranes now number over 400 wild birds, up from a low of 15 in 1941. Long before this trip, I did some research on viewing the birds from a boat and found a local fishing captain who could help. There was no guarantee of seeing a crane since they range over many thousands of acres, much of it off limits to powerboats. Though we were confined to the periphery of the refuge, we came upon a pond where a pair of cranes and some spoonbills were feeding.

Page218 Heermann's Gull & Sea Lion
Monterey, California
(January 2003) *Nikon
F5, 600mm f4 lens
with 2x TC,
Kodak E100 VS*

Monterey was a must-see as Kristie and I worked our way up the coast. The day before, we stopped at 17-Mile Drive to take in California sea lions hauled out on "Birdrock." Morning light would be more flattering, so we returned at daybreak to behold the monolith covered with sea lions from top-to-bottom. What you see in this photo is merely the top of the rock. Upwards of several hundred sea lions were basking that morning, with many dozens swimming below. I framed in a bit of sky for birds to pass through to complete the composition. I was able to photograph pelicans, cormorants and even a Snowy Egret, but this frame balanced well with a pair of Heermann's Gulls.

Page219, 220 Pelicans & Cormorants
La Jolla, California (January 2001) *Nikon F5, 600mm f4 lens, Kodak E100 VS*

Concerning the cormorants, the four birds on the right are Brandt's Cormorants, strictly a West Coast species. The bird on the far left is a Double-crested Cormorant, found across the continent. The main attraction at the cliffs of La Jolla are the Western Brown Pelicans who roost peacefully alongside both species of cormorant and a few varieties of gull. Perched birds rarely keep the head still, preferring to scan their surroundings for possible danger. I remember waiting a good while with these birds until each individual provided a side view of the bill. The beautiful blue background is the Pacific Ocean. With multiple birds, I stop down my aperture to increase depth-of-field.

Page219 Western Gull and Elephant Seal
San Simeon, California
(January 2003) *Nikon
F100, 28-200 f4.5 lens,
Fuji Velvia 50*

As Kristie and I headed north to Monterey, I recalled a great shoot in 1999 at Point Piedras Blancas, just south of the Hearst Castle. During the winter months, elephant seals give birth on these protected beaches. Gulls flock to harvest the nutritious afterbirth. Having missed a feeding frenzy in 1999, I was hopeful for one on this trip, even though we only had one morning to visit here. Kristie and I worked the smaller beach to the right of the parking lot where you are very close to the action. Over the course of two hours, we were blessed to see three births and gulls feasting aplenty. I was so close that I popped on the 28-200 mm zoom and shot from maybe 40 feet away.

Page220 Black-crowned Night-Heron
Mission Bay, California
(January 2001) *Nikon F100,
80-400 f4.5 zoom lens,
Fuji Provia 100*

We visited Paradise Point Resort on San Diego's Mission Bay to photograph the very tame resident ducks. I started up a conversation with a hotel staffer while shooting at the main pond next to the lobby. They were kind enough to tell me of a Black-crowned Night-Heron who hung out at the outdoor café facing Mission Bay. Apparently, he had a fondness for chicken, according to the sympathetic wait staff. We found three herons... word had gotten out about the free chicken. This adult was perched in a palm tree by the entrance. The sun was just about to set and the palm fronds were lit beautifully, screaming out for a habitat portrait.

Page220 Whimbrel
Carmel, California
(January 1999) *Nikon
F5, 600mm f4 lens
with 1.4x TC,
Fuji Provia 100*

This morning, I arrived at Point Lobos at sunrise, hoping to photograph Black Oystercatchers. I assumed incorrectly that the sanctuary would open at dawn like most parks. It didn't take me long to figure out Plan B. I had just passed a nice stretch of beach in south Carmel, where surely there ought to be birds. I parked at a posh hillside neighborhood and started out making crashing wave photos (page 16) with my 600mm telephoto. Off to the sandy beach, I discovered a lone Whimbrel feeding in the sand. We played cat & mouse for a good while before working out a mutually acceptable working distance. At this point, I was able to make a number of photos of this stunning shorebird.

Page221 Ring-billed Gulls
Coronado Beach,
California (January 2001)
*Nikon F5, 80-400 f4.5
lens, Kodak E100 VS*

This beautiful stretch of beach near the landmark Hotel del Coronado is a regular stop for Arthur Morris on his Southern California photo tours that I have attended twice. The main objective is flying gulls. After a productive session, we all hung out to take in the sunset. As the sun dropped, the colors kept intensifying. I was concerned about the dim light since I didn't have a tripod with me. I would have to rely on the vibration-reduction technology of my new 80-400 zoom lens. Shooting at a wide-open aperture, I managed a shutter speed of 1/30 of a second handheld. To my surprise, most of the shots were sharp. Moments later, the gulls departed from the beach for their nighttime roost.

Page222 Black-legged Kittiwakes
Cape St. Mary's, Newfoundland (July 1999) *Nikon N90s, 24mm f2.8 lens, Fuji Velvia 50*

Trite as it may sound, the scenery is breathtaking at Cape St. Mary's, anchoring Newfoundland's Avalon Peninsula. We were very fortunate in that the fog was minimal during our one-day visit. I heard stories of people traveling to the cape several times and never getting a clear view of Birdrock, the main gannet colony just offshore. In this sweeping wide-angle view, you get a real sense of place, from the lichen-encrusted rocks along the cliffs to the distant lighthouse near the parking area. Most of the white specks you see here are Black-legged Kittiwakes that nest in abundance. The regal Northern Gannet also flies by regularly. One is visible near the top of this frame.

Page224 Least Grebe
San Christobal River, Mexico (December 2000) *Nikon F100, 80-400mm f4.5 lens, Kodak E100 VS*

Although I had photographed the Least Grebe in Texas and the Bahamas, I didn't have any pictures that excited me. When I booked a jungle boat tour of the lush San Christobal River near San Blas, I didn't realize that we would be seeing any grebes here. When doing bird photography from a boat, I try to book the boat for myself, so that the captain can work with me when good opportunities arise. We were cruising along when this tiny diver popped up right by the boat. We killed the motor and watched as he fished around us. When the bird swam into a shaded section of vegetation, I attached the strobe and shot flash as main light.

Page226 Wood Duck
Patterson Park, Maryland (September 2000) *Nikon F5, 600mm f4 lens, Kodak E100 VS*

Over a three-year period, I shot thousands of pictures of wild Wood Ducks in Baltimore City, where several pairs graced the Boat Lake. I had always wanted shots of woodies perched on logs. I got permission from the park supervisor to anchor a variety of perches in the lake. A lovely sycamore branch that came down in a windstorm caught my attention. I heaved it 30 feet onto an existing anchored log and it landed perfectly, forming an arch over the main perch. If I had 100 chances to throw that branch again to land in that exact position for a million dollars, I doubt that I could even come close to my lucky throw. This arch was meant to frame this hen. She revealed her blue speculum for one picture.

Page230 Horned Puffin
Pribilof Islands, Alaska (July 1998) *Nikon N90s, Tokina 400mm f5.6 lens, Fuji Sensia 100*

This is the one species of seabird that was proving elusive for a nice portrait. All the ones I had seen were perched too far away. On the far corner of the island, we were exploring a popular cliff for birds perched near the top, the only place to shoot from. I finally found this lovely puffin, but the view was obstructed. That's the real challenge here in the Pribilofs—finding clear views into the birds perched beneath you. It dawned on me that if I lay on my belly and inched out, I could circumvent a distracting clump of grass. I was a bit uneasy leaning over the top of a 150 foot cliff with a handheld telephoto. All of this "living on the edge" stuff was new to me in 1998.

Page223 Razorbill
Machias Seal Island, Maine (July 2001) *Nikon F100, 80-400 f4.5 lens, Fuji Provia 100*

I was very hopeful of seeing the Razorbill, a bird of the North Atlantic that had eluded me two years earlier in Newfoundland. John Norton, who runs trips out to the island with his father, Barna, assured me that I would make its acquaintance. Once you land on the island via zodiacs (waves permitting), you are escorted to a staging area for instructions about minimizing impact amidst all the nesting seabirds. Pictures are only allowed from the photo blinds that have holes cut out on all sides. This massive boulder was maybe fifty feet from one of the blinds. My close-ups of the Razorbills were disappointing since the black eye can get lost in the black face. This scenic distant shot worked out the best.

Page224 Boat-billed & Bare-throated Tiger Heron
San Christobal River, Mexico (December 2000) *Nikon F5, 600mm f4 lens, Fuji Provia 100*

The main reason for booking a boat ride through mangrove swamps was to photograph these two tropical herons. Common in Mexico, they don't venture north of the border. Our experienced guide knew of a likely set of trees where the reclusive Boat-billed Heron would rest. Sure enough, several birds were tucked away in the tangle of branches. It was very challenging to find a clean angle on a bird. We saw two tiger herons before this one, but they spooked before any shots could be made. With great fortune, a third was spotted in a tree some distance from the bank. I asked the captain if I could deboard and have a go of it, which he allowed.

Page227 Tundra Swans
Magothy River, Maryland (February 1999) *Nikon F5, 28-200mm f4.5 lens, Kodak E100 VS*

I am blessed to live so close to the Chesapeake Bay. This magnet for wintering waterfowl, like the Tundra Swan, has enthralled me since my first sighting as a child. A large group of swans travels thousands of miles from the tundra in northern Canada and Alaska to this river on the bay each autumn. They spend the entire winter here feeding on aquatic vegetation and handouts of corn. By returning to the same dock on many occasions, I increase my chances of seeing a glorious sunrise like this one. Some days, the birds stay out on the river until well after sunrise. On this particular morning, they were already waiting for me when I arrived to start feeding.

Page230 Northern Fulmar
Pribilof Islands, Alaska (July 1998) *Nikon F5, 600mm f4 lens, Fuji Sensia 100*

The Northern Fulmar was the easiest species to catch in flight on St. Paul Island. They soared for hours on end near the clifftops, but getting a perched shot proved to be difficult. This was my first photo tour with Arthur Morris and he was pivotal in making this shot possible. Wandering off to explore different angles, he found a very nice look from a grassy ledge into a fulmar roost. After shooting some, he kindly offered his position to me for the only clear view into the crevice. Up until this project, nature photography was very much a solitary pursuit for me. I've learned that through teamwork, wildlife photographers can enhance the experience for everyone by being generous.

Page223 Atlantic Puffin
Machias Seal Island, Maine (July 2001) *Nikon F5, 300mm f4 lens, Kodak E100 VS*

I was determined to have the classic puffin shot with a beak stuffed with fish. When I booked the trip a few months prior, I was told that July is a good month to get puffins perched with fish. From my blind, I was very disappointed to see that everytime a bird landed with fish, it would immediately retreat into the burrow to feed the young. On the third day of shooting, I concentrated on getting a flight shot with fish in the bill. These are speedy little birds, making flight shots daunting. I had to use a short telephoto lens as the portals were too small to maneuver the big lens. The key was getting one to land right near the blind. I stood at the ready for my entire 45-minute shoot and got three flight sequences.

Page225 Magnificent Frigatebird
Isabel Island, Mexico (December 2000) *Nikon F5, 600mm f4 lens with 1.4x TC, Fuji Provia 100*

This frigatebird nest was unapproachable, centered in a study area monitored by Dutch biologists. From the viewing area, a dilapidated military shelter, my view was obstructed. The day before, I noticed several perched male green iguanas. I hoped for a combination shot with a frigate nest on my last day. Low and behold, this handsome fellow was perched right below the nest, but the shrubs blocked my view. I needed a ladder to get ten feet higher for a clear view. Biologists searched amidst the ruins and found an old ladder for me to rest against a decrepit cinder block wall. I climbed up and anchored my monopod on a ladder rung while sitting on a single row of cinder blocks.

Page228 Crested Auklet & Tufted Puffin
Pribilof Islands, Alaska (July 1998) *Nikon F5, 600mm f4 lens, Fuji Sensia 100*

In case you hadn't figured it out, these are two different photographs made to appear as one image by printing them side-by-side. The implication is quite valid in that a variety of nesting seabirds will perch in close proximity where prime ledges are concentrated. It's tempting to shoot tight on a beautiful bird. I have trained myself over the years to pull back when the surrounding scenery warrants. Here, the rocks are so beautiful and integral to the birds' presence that I opted to step back. In both images, having a sliver of ocean background really helps out, creating a visual break from the detailed rocks. If you look carefully, a small Least Auklet is perched just above the Crested Auklet.

Page230 Red-faced Cormorant
Pribilof Islands, Alaska (July 1998) *Nikon F5, 600mm f4 lens, Fuji Sensia 100*

Having seen hundreds of Double-crested Cormorants on my travels, what a strange experience to see a cormorant with a bright red facemask. When you journey to the continent's far perimeter, all sorts of unusual things show up. Our group of five shooters was approaching a cliff when this bird appeared from behind a rock. Because the cliffs are such a big part of the scenery, I framed in some rocks on the right side to convey a sense of place. Had I moved several paces to the left, I could have had a solid blue background. This image was taken after dinner, maybe 10 p.m. One of the odd things about shooting here in summer is that the sun sets well after midnight.

Photography Notes

Page231 Parakeet Auklet & Least Auklet
Pribilof Islands, Alaska (July 1998) *Nikon F5, 600mm f4 lens, Fuji Sensia 100*

Almost all of the seabirds on St. Paul Island perched as pairs or singles, so I was inspired upon finding three Parakeet Auklets together. There was a great deal of interaction; perhaps a straggler was testing the bond of an established pair. I tried to capture the tension of the moment when the birds stared at each other. Moments later, there was vigorous wing flapping that my lens was too tight for. One of the things that really impressed me was how the auklets could perch on a nearly vertical wall, gripping a crack in the rock. The Least Auklet is a tiny seabird, about the size of a robin. For this one, I simply waited for the head to profile to click my portrait.

Page231 Thick-billed Murre
Pribilof Islands, Alaska (July 1998) *Nikon F5, 600mm f4 lens, Fuji Sensia 100*

There's a small cliff area next to the main fur seal colony where a handful of birds roost on lovely perches. Unfortunately, there are only a few vantage points to work from, a problem when on a group shoot. Here, I got my best shots of the Thick-billed Murre with a pair nestled together on a tiny ledge. Seabirds here lay oblong eggs that can only roll in a tight circle and not over the edge. This species is a challenge to successfully photograph since the dark eye blends in with the dark face. The light must hit the birds at just the right angle for catchlight in the eye. These birds were constantly moving their heads to look in various directions.

Page232 Stilt Sandpiper & Red-necked Phalarope
Churchill, Canada (June 1998) *Nikon F5, 600mm f4 lens with 1.4x TC, Fuji Sensia 100*

A large lake near town was reported to host nesting Pacific Loons, so our group of five shooters led by Moose Peterson hiked to our jewel at the opposite lakeshore. On the way, we encountered various shorebirds in the shallows. The tiny Red-necked Phalarope is a highly active bird when feeding. Just when you think you have the moment, she turns away and there is no shot. One has to wait for the bird to pause between feeding sorties. Along the same trail, we encountered a Stilt Sandpiper whose very long legs are partially submerged in this frame. This shorebird is a common nester on the tundra, but this is the only one we saw on the only sunny day in a week of exploring.

Page232 Hudsonian Godwit
Churchill, Canada (June 1998) *Nikon F5, 600mm f4 lens with 1.4x TC, Fuji Sensia 100*

Much of our time in Churchill was spent in the van driven by our guide Moose Peterson. With five sets of eyes scouring the tundra, we pulled over frequently to investigate bird sightings. Many times, the birds would disappear in the tall grass or would flush when approached by a group of lensmen. The goal was to find a nest, giving a bird a reason to hang around. We passed this fellow and I asked Moose to pull over, so I could have a go at it. Other members of the group were frustrated with the difficulty in finding willing subjects and had lost their drive. I recall being the only photographer to approach the bird on foot, which probably helped to not scare him off.

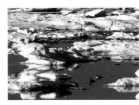

Page233 Common Eider
Churchill, Canada (June 1998) *Nikon F5, 600mm f4 lens with 1.4x TC, Fuji Sensia 100*

My favorite place to photograph in Churchill was the Cape, which provided a stunning view of the Hudson Bay filled with icebergs. We visited several times during the week-long adventure and occasionally sea ducks could be spotted resting on the ice. Getting close-ups was not an option as they consistently swam away when approached. At this moment, I was working arctic hares foraging on sparse tundra vegetation. Gazing out to sea, I saw this pair of Common Eiders approaching. A great habitat shot was unfolding; I just needed to compose and click when the birds were clearly visible between the ice. I was careful not to center my subject to enhance the composition.

Page233 Parasitic Jaeger
Churchill, Canada (June 1998) *Nikon F5, 600mm f4 lens with 1.4x TC, Fuji Sensia 100*

At the outset of *Rhapsody*, it was a great thrill to travel to exotic locations where virtually all of the species would be new to me. The Parasitic Jaeger was an alluring target, a pirate that raids other seabirds carrying fish. Moose heard of a nest location and we marched a great distance across the tundra to find it. Before we got close enough for nest shots, the incubating adult took wing and circled overhead. Had this been an overcast day, there would have been no pictures as gray skies are awful for flight shots. This was the only flight shooting I did that week. After a few passes we decided to back off, so the bird could return to incubating. Even in summer it can be bitter cold and the eggs need to stay warm for proper development.

Page234 Snow Geese & Sandhill Crane
Bosque del Apache NWR, New Mexico (November 1998) *Nikon N90s, 300mm f4.5 lens, Fuji Velvia 50*

As much as I love this shot, I have to be honest and say this moment is not extraordinary at Bosque, where birds light up the landscape at every turn. When grain is harvested in late autumn, thousands of birds descend on the farm fields to reap the bounty. At any given time, some flocks are moving into the area while others are moving out. The 300mm telephoto I brought along was the perfect focal length to frame in the mountains and sky. Because of overcast skies, I selected Velvia to brighten up the landscape. That same afternoon, I watched a pair of coyotes hunting this field for compromised birds. As long as the coyotes kept a distance, the birds remained calm.

Page236 Snow Geese
Bosque del Apache NWR, New Mexico (November 1998) *Nikon N90s, 300mm f4.5 lens, Fuji Velvia 50*

During my first visit to Bosque, I was reliant on Arthur Morris as our tour group leader to put us in the best positions possible throughout the day. He has been shooting here so long that he knows how to work the refuge for maximum success. We set up before sunrise by this huge impoundment where geese spend the night, out of reach to land predators. I was really drawn to the lavender water reflecting the dawn sky, a great backdrop for snow-white birds. Some birds were already flying and they blurred against the mountains at a slow shutter speed. After fumbling with my old tripod head on this shoot, I decided to invest in the flexible Whimberly system for future trips.

Page237 Sandhill Crane
Bosque del Apache NWR, New Mexico (November 2000) *Nikon F5, 600mm f4 lens with 1.4x TC, Kodak E100 VS*

On my second Bosque trip, there was something very different from the first visit in 1998. Hundreds of Sandhill Cranes had taken to a new pond just outside the refuge entrance. In late afternoon, they would fly in to spend the night. By sunrise, small groups would leave a few at a time. As the sun came up, there were still plenty of birds bathed in sweet, golden light. When doing group shots, it helps for the eye to have a focal point, something that stands out to lead your eye into the shot. I'm always looking for one or two birds to become the focus of attention even if they are still small in the frame. Cranes are highly animated creatures, so I didn't have to wait long for action.

Page237 Yellow-headed Blackbird
Bosque Del Apache NWR, New Mexico (November 1998) *Nikon N90s, 600mm f4 lens with 2x TC, Fuji Sensia 100*

Before this trip, I had never seen a Yellow-headed Blackbird. When this flock alighted on a tree near the wildlife drive, I was surprised to see such bright color in the desert. Perhaps 200 individuals covered the naked branches along with a sprinkling of Red-winged Blackbirds. A red wing patch is barely visible in the lower left portion of the composition. Instead of moving in close and possibly spooking the birds, I popped on my 2x teleconverter to get in tight. I was able to work both vertical and horizontal frames for several minutes before the flock took off. Though waterbirds are the main attraction, all kinds of birds show up at this desert oasis.

Page267 Great Egret
St. Augustine, Florida (April 1999) *Nikon F5, 600mm f4 lens, Fuji Provia 100*

Watching a particular egret nest on this trip, I got the idea for framing chicks with a cascade of mom's courtship plumes. Though most photographs are very static, the activity in this nest was anything but. The chicks were constantly moving about the nest, jockeying for position under a feeding parent. The key for this shot was being able to get the adult's head in the frame. I couldn't back up on the boardwalk anymore, so the parent would have to bend over to fit the head in. Another challenge was to see all of the chicks framed between the legs... a very tall order, but not out of the question if one is patient. Over a three-day shoot, I stood vigil by the nest for at least five hours, loving every second of it.

Page268 Cormorants & Gulls
Monterey, California (January 1999) *Nikon N90s, 600mm f4 lens, Fuji Sensia 100*

In my teens, I traveled to California with my parents and Monterey's 17-Mile Drive made quite an impression, especially "Birdrock" where sea lions would haul out. When I scheduled a California trip in 1999, I made sure to put Monterey on the itinerary. We arrived before sunset on our first visit. Needless to say, it was hard to make out the sea lions on the distant shaded rock. Strong winds were kicking up large waves that periodically crashed into Birdrock. Larger waves would force perched birds to take flight. When the sunset intensified, I was eager for that special wave to knock a few birds off their perches for a dramatic habitat shot. There are a handful of basking sea lions in the shadows.

Also from Ravenwood Press

The Miracle Pond

Over a five-year period Maryland photographer Middleton Evans made over 400 missions to Patterson Park, documenting an astounding 110 bird species. Just minutes from downtown Baltimore, this 155-acre sports & recreation complex features a small lake, home to nesting Wood Ducks. A dream come true, Evans was able to document nearly every aspect of their life cycle—a real challenge for this highly secretive species. Another 30 kinds of waterbirds also gifted incredible moments to the camera. The project expanded upon encountering a friendly Yellow-bellied Sapsucker; over the next three years nearly 70 species of songbirds and a few raptors would reveal themselves in the canopy. In 2002 the lake was completely drained and renovated, leaving the woodies and other waterbirds homeless for a year... would any return? This volume of 400 compelling images tells a vivid story of nature's abundance in an unlikely setting. Available from Ravenwood Press in the fall of 2008

PO Box 496
Fallston, Maryland 21047-0496
Phone 1-800-807-1079 / Fax 410-877-2419
www.ravenwoodpress.com

Maryland's Great Outdoors

From the Appalachian Mountains to the Atlantic beaches, Maryland has earned the nickname "America in Miniature." For twenty years, Middleton Evans has dedicated his career to photographing his home state's diverse cultural and natural scenery. A mere two hundred miles wide, this ninth smallest state is remarkably endowed with plant and animal life harbored in unique habitats. Wild orchids, carnivorous bog plants, mysterious forest creatures, regal birds of prey and dazzling butterflies... these are just some of the treasures encountered over four years of exploring Maryland's wild places. With nearly three hundred photographs, *Maryland's Great Outdoors* is a compelling collection that lifts the spirit with the glory and majesty of Creation.

Fine Art Prints

Select images from *Rhapsody in Blue* are available as limited edition giclee prints. Please visit the *Rhapsody in Blue* gallery at www.ravenwoodpress.com for ordering information.

Mission Statement

Ravenwood Press was born on the Salisbury Plains of southern England as Middleton and Kristie Evans traveled to Stonehenge in December 2004. A poignant moment with a pair of ravens by the visitor's center signaled that it was time to take action and form a publishing company to share compelling photography and soul-stirring stories in coffee table books and calendars. Though a variety of topics will be explored, from Maryland-related themes to the wonders of Nature, the stories will all boil down to one essential message—the infinite grace, beauty and love of God. We believe that God has blessed each person with a set of talents and gifts as unique as a fingerprint. When properly nourished and expressed, these skills serve as a conduit for God's grace to uplift others in need. We hope that our publications inspire others to continue their journey towards maturing as beacons of light for a world starved of love, compassion and forgiveness.

References

Several books were especially helpful during my research for *Rhapsody in Blue*. They include *The Birder's Handbook: A Field Guide to the Natural History of North American Birds*, by Paul Ehrlich, David S. Dobkin and Dayl Wheye; *The Sibley Guide to Bird Life & Behavior*, by David Allen Sibley; *Lives of North American Birds*, by Kenn Kaufman; *Waterbirds of the Northeast*, by Winston Williams; and *The Art of Bird Photography*, by Arthur Morris.

Permissions

Technical Notes

All the photographs in this collection were made on Nikon F3, F5, N90s and F100 bodies. Nikkor lenses include the 600mm AF-S f4, 300mm AF-S f2.8, 300mm AF-S f4, 80-400mm AF VR f4.5-5.6, 28-200 AF f3.5-5.6, 105mm f2.8, and 24mm f2.8. Both the 1.4x and 2x Nikon teleconverters were used extensively. On occasion a Gitzo carbon fiber tripod was used in combination with a Whimberley head. The majority of photographs were shot on a Manfrotto monopod with a pivot head for added flexibility with action photography. Staple films for the project include Kodak E100 VS, Fuji Sensia 100, Fuji Provia 100, Fuji Velvia 50, and Fuji RMS 100-1000. Nearly all of the film was push-processed 1 stop, either at home with a Jobo Autolab or by Chelsea Color Lab in New York. All the images were scanned on the Nikon Coolscan 5000 and 8000 models, output through Adobe Photoshop CS2 by Harrison Photographic (www.harrison-photo.com). Adjustments were made with contrast, color balance, shadow details and sharpness in a few cases. In a few instances additional edge (sky or water) was cloned when a moving subject was too tight on the edge.

Index

Rhap·so·dy (răp′ sə-dē) n., pl. **-dies** 1. Exalted or excessively enthusiastic expression of feeling in speech or writing. 2. A literary work written in an impassioned or exalted style. 3. *Mus.* A composition of irregular form and an often improvisatory character. 4. In ancient Greece, an epic poem or a portion of one suitable for uninterrupted recitation.

Travel Log

1 Barrow
2 Nome
3 St. Paul Island
4 Anchorage Lakes
5 Homer-Spit
6 Middleton Island
7 Cannon Beach
8 Off Newport
9 North Santiam
10 Bodega Bay
11 Lake Meritt
12 Palo Alto Baylands
13 Carmel
14 Point Lobos
15 San Simeon
16 Santa Barbara
17 Bolsa Chica
18 Upper Newport Bay
19 Santee Lakes
20 La Jolla
21 Mission Bay
22 Coronado Island
23 Chula Vista
24 Isabel Island
25 San Christobal River
26 Bosque Del Apache
27 Soccoro Pond
28 Corpus Christi
29 Mustang Island
30 Port Aransas
31 Aransas NWR
32 Brazos Bend
33 Bolivar Flats
34 Wakulla Springs
35 St. Mark's NWR
36 Bradenton Dock
37 Sarasota Bay
38 Myakka River
39 Oscar Scherer Park

40 Venice Rookery
41 Placida
42 Sanibel Island
43 Estero Lagoon
44 Three Lakes Park
45 Cork Screw Swamp
46 Anhinga Trail
47 Pericles' Pond
48 Great Inagua
49 Loxahatchee NWR
50 Wakodahatchee Wetlands
51 Lake Kissimmee
52 Merritt Island NWR
53 St. Augustine Rookery
54 Assateague Island
55 Ocean City Jetty
56 Deal Island
57 Tred Avon River
58 Magothy River
59 Patterson Park
60 Druid Hill Park
61 Bear Branch Park
62 Aberdeen
63 Port Mahon
64 Cape May
65 Stone Harbor
66 Jamaica Bay
67 Lake Alamoosook
68 Machias Seal Island
69 Cape Saint Mary's
70 St. John's
71 Cape Bonavista
72 Churchill
73 Lake Manitoba
74 Alonsa District
75 Three Mile Lake
76 Hennepin Parks
77 Benton Lakes
78 Freezeout Lake